For Debo, a national treasure,
with affection and admiration.

Contents

Introduction

WILL I ALWAYS FEEL too embarrassed to say I am English? I was born in the world. I was born in Europe. I was born in Britain. I was born in England. All these statements are true. But if you ask me my country of origin, it is England.

My great-grandmother was Scottish. I have a kilt. And yet when I wore it to a formal dinner a few months ago, a lady with a pronounced Scottish accent, having enquired about my ancestry, declared that I had no right to wear tartan. 'Far too long ago,' she snorted, and turned on her heel and left before she could see my blushes. I haven't had the courage to wear it since. So perhaps I must settle for being British and leave national pride to the Scots, the Irish and the Welsh. The pure-breeds.

But what, then, would happen to England? It won't just disappear. It has to exist as a name for the bits that don't belong to Scotland, Ireland and Wales. So as it's here, I might as well own up to being part of it.

And there you have it, the classic English trait – the ability to apologise even when we have not done anything wrong.

We are as good at that as we are at queuing, watching Wimbledon in the rain and having nice gardens.

So this little book is a celebration of some of the things that are English. Things that we can be proud of, rather than apologise for. You will find that there are lots of things that are not in it. There's not much about football, but then I don't see why eleven men I don't know should dictate my mood of a weekend. There is even less about *The Bill* or *EastEnders*. I don't like them much. But there is a bit about *The Archers*. And about how to make the perfect cup of tea, and scones and jam and clotted cream, and nursery rhymes, and Gilbert and Sullivan, and Alan Bennett and Alfred Wainwright. I like them.

I suppose my England is shot through with nostalgia, and sentimentality, with authors like Jane Austen and Charles Dickens, Laurie Lee and Beatrix Potter. There are bits about love and about childhood, about food and about the Royal Family.

I do have a ridiculous love of this country, having seen most of it over the years – from the cliffs of Cornwall to the Yorkshire Dales, from the Essex marshes to the Norfolk Broads, from the Fens and the Black Country to the Lincolnshire Wolds and the windswept beaches of Northumberland.

There are snippets of this and that which will give anyone coming to this country for the first time an idea of the sort of place we live in; the sort of people we are. Or were. Our history is, after all, a part of what we are today – more than those things that have only just happened and which might fade into oblivion in a few years' time. You could accuse *England, Our England* of being a bit old-fashioned in its outlook; but then so am I. It must be something to do with being English. So I'm sorry.

Alan Titchmarsh

This Scepter'd Isle

This royal throne of kings, this scepter'd isle,
This earth of majesty, this seat of Mars,
This other Eden, demi-paradise,
This fortress built by Nature for herself
Against infection and the hand of war,
This happy breed of men, this little world,
This precious stone set in the silver sea,
Which serves it in the office of a wall
Or as a moat defensive to a house,
Against the envy of less happier lands,
This blessèd plot, this earth, this realm, this England.

Richard II, Act II, Scene 1,
William Shakespeare (1564–1616)

The Kings and Queens of England

A WIT ONCE REMARKED that in a few years' time there will only be five royal families left: hearts, clubs, diamonds, spades and Windsor. He may well be right. But the Windsors (a family name adopted by King George V to pacify a country who found his German Saxe-Coburg-Gotha roots unsettling in times of national strife) are only the last in a long line of English kings and queens – though few of them were born here.

House of Wessex

802–39	Egbert
839–58	Aethelwulf (son of Egbert)
858–60	Aethelbald (first son of Aethelwulf)
860–65	Aethelberht (second son of Aethelwulf)
865–71	Aethelred I (third son of Aethelwulf)
871–99	Alfred, the Great (fourth son of Aethelwulf)
899–924	Edward, the Elder (son of Alfred)
924–39	Athelstan (first son of Edward the Elder)
939–46	Edmund I, the Magnificent (second son of Edward the Elder)
946–55	Eadred (third son of Edward the Elder)
955–59	Eadwig, the Fair (first son of Edmund)
959–75	Edgar, the Peaceable (second son of Edmund)
975–78	Edward, the Martyr (first son of Edgar)
978–1013 and 1014–16	Ethelred II, the Unready (second son of Edgar)
1016	Edmund II, Ironside (222 days; son of Ethelred II)

Danish Kings

1013–14	Sweyn, Forkbeard
1016–35	Canute (son of Sweyn Forkbeard)
1035–40	Harold I, Harefoot (first son of Canute)
1040–42	Harthacanute (second son of Canute)

House of Wessex (restored)

1042–66   Edward, the Confessor (son of Ethelred II)
1066   Harold II (283 days; Harold Godwinson, son of Godwin, Earl of Wessex)

Norman Kings

1066–87   William I, the Conqueror (son of Robert I, the Magnificent, Duke of Normandy)
1087–1100 William II, Rufus (son of William I)
1100–35   Henry I, Beauclerc (son of William II)
1135–54   Stephen (nephew of Henry I)

Plantagenet Kings

HOUSE OF ANGEVIN

1154–89   Henry II, Curtmantle (grandson of Henry I)
1189–99   Richard I, the Lionheart (third son of Henry II)
1199–1216 John, Lackland (fifth son of Henry II)
1216–72   Henry III (son of John)
1272–1307 Edward I, Longshanks (son of Henry III)
1307–27   Edward II (son of Edward I)
1327–77   Edward III (son of Edward II)
1377–99   Richard II (son of the Black Prince, grandson of Edward III)

HOUSE OF LANCASTER

1399–1413   Henry IV, Bolingbroke (son of John of Gaunt,
            grandson of Edward III)
1413–22   Henry V (son of Henry IV)
1422–61 and 1470–71
            Henry VI (son of Henry V)

HOUSE OF YORK

1461–70 and 1471–83
            Edward IV (eldest surviving son of Richard, Duke
            of York)
1483   Edward V (two months; eldest son of Edward IV)
1483–85   Richard III, Crookback (youngest son of Richard,
            Duke of York)

House of Tudor

1485–1509   Henry VII (son of Edmund Tudor and Margaret
            Beaufort, great-great-granddaughter of Edward III)
1509–47   Henry VIII (second son of Henry VII)
1547–53   Edward VI (Henry's son by Jane Seymour)
1553   Lady Jane Grey (nine days; daughter of Henry Grey,
            Duke of Suffolk)
1553–58   Mary I (Henry's daughter by Catherine of Aragon)
1558–1603   Elizabeth I (Henry's daughter by Anne Boleyn)

House of Stuart

1603–25   James I (James VI of Scotland; great-great-grandson of Henry VII)

1625–49   Charles I (second son of James)

Commonwealth

1649–58   Oliver Cromwell, Lord Protector

1658–59   Richard Cromwell

House of Stuart (restored)

1660–85   Charles II (eldest son of Charles I)

1685–88   James II (brother of Charles II)

House of Orange and Stuart

1689–94   William (grandson of Charles I) and Mary II (daughter of James II)

1694–1702 William III (after Mary's death)

House of Stuart

1702–14   Anne (sister of Mary)

House of Hanover

1714–27   George I (great-grandson of James I)

1727–60   George II (son of George I)
1760–1820   George III (grandson of George II)
1820–30   George IV (son of George III; Prince Regent from
                    1811)
1830–37   William IV (brother of George IV)
1837–1901   Victoria (niece of William IV)

House of Saxe-Coburg-Gotha

1901–10   Edward VII (eldest son of Victoria and Prince Albert)

House of Windsor

1910–36   George V (second son of Edward VII)
1936–52   George VI (second son of George V on abdication
                    of his elder brother, who would have been
                    Edward VIII had he been crowned)
1952–   Elizabeth II (elder daughter of George VI)

I was taught a kind of theoretic republicanism which was prepared to tolerate a monarch so long as he recognised that he was an employee of the people and subject to dismissal if he proved unsatisfactory. My grandfather, who was no respecter of persons, used to explain this point of view to Queen Victoria, and she was not altogether sympathetic.

Portraits From Memory (1956),
Bertrand Russell (1872–1970)

The lion and the unicorn
Were fighting for the crown;
The lion beat the unicorn
All about the town.
Some gave them white bread,
And some gave them brown;
Some gave them plum cake,
And sent them out of town.

'The Lion and the Unicorn' (date unknown),
Anon.

Tea With the Queen

MANY PEOPLE DREAM of having tea with the Queen. But in order to stand the slightest chance of sipping from Her Majesty's finest bone china, you will need to introduce yourself first. And the only way to do that is to write her a letter. But bear in mind that there is an etiquette that must be observed when addressing our monarch. Take notice and you will avoid coming to grief. Or going to the Tower.

Begin the letter with 'Madam' or 'May it please Your Majesty', and end it with 'I have the honour to remain, Madam, Your Majesty's humble and obedient servant'.

In the unlikely event that your letter succeeds in persuading the Queen to invite you to Buckingham Palace, you should address her as 'Your Majesty' the first time you speak to her, and subsequently as 'Ma'am'. Courtiers will tell you that the word should rhyme with 'jam' not 'farm', and try not to use it in every sentence or it becomes monotonous and rather sycophantic. When you first enter the room, men should bow (just from the neck, not from the waist) and women should execute a bob curtsy (put one leg behind the other and bend slightly at the knees, gently bowing the head at the same time.

There is no need to hold your skirt out). It's a good idea to practice on a friend beforehand to avoid falling over. That said, the Queen has indicated that this is no longer essential protocol, but it's a nice touch all the same and shows that you care about these things.

And then Unity Hall and Ingrid Seward have helpful advice on how proceedings might unfold:

The Royal Family and their guests still change for tea; the women take off their tweeds and put on something like a pretty silk dress, and the men, after tramping the fields all day, change into a pair of flannel trousers and a favourite cashmere pullover. The room in which they eat tea is worth dressing up for. Everyone is surrounded by the Queen's Fabergé collection: cases and cases of it, and worth a Queen's ransom.

When Sandringham is full, there are usually fourteen for tea; the Queen sits at one end of the table, her lady-in-waiting at the other. There is no formal seating arrangement, so by arriving well in time it's possible to stake a claim on the seat next to Her Majesty.

She is very much in charge at teatime. In front of her is a silver kettle with an ivory handle, which sits on a stand with a paraffin burner beneath. The kettle itself tips forward to pour, and it looks like a rather dangerous arrangement. The contraption is supposed to be balanced, and as they have been using the same kettle since Queen Victoria's days and there is no family history of anyone being scalded, presumably it must be safer than it looks. In front of the Queen is a silver salver holding a Victorian silver teapot and a china milk jug and sugar bowl. Placed by these is a very long, thin piece of silver that looks like a fine trumpet. Her Majesty blows through this delicately when she wants to extinguish the burner.

She has two tea caddies at her elbow, one containing her own royal blend, and the other, Indian tea. The Queen's special blend is a mixture of China and Indian tea. Made by Twining's, it is packed in a square tin, and is not exclusive to the Royal Family. Anyone can buy it from Fortnum and Mason's.

With all the implements of the afternoon ritual set in place, the Queen herself warms the teapot – considered an absolute necessity to produce a really good cuppa. When she decides the pot is nicely warmed she pours the water she used for the job into a small basin that holds the tea-strainer. A hovering page then empties this. She spoons the tea into the pot with a silver spoon, and adds boiling water from her silver kettle. It is doubtful if the Queen has ever seen a teabag, and she would probably not know what to do with it if she did.

On the Queen's right are six cups. She serves only the top end of her table; her lady-in-waiting is going through the same tea-making ritual at the other end, with the same sort of silver kettle, and will serve those nearest to her. If there are more than usual for tea, extra cups are placed on a small side table at the Queen's elbow. She pours and then passes the cups down the table, serving herself last. For some reason the men always get large breakfast cups, while the ladies are given little ones. Prince Philip never pours – it is considered woman's work. Sugar bowls containing lump sugar with silver tongs are ranged along the length of the table, and there is, of course, a choice of milk or lemon.

The teapot empty, the page comes in with an ordinary electric kettle full of boiling water. This modern but necessary accoutrement is kept outside, out of sight, and the page boils it as needed and replenishes the water in the Queen's silver kettle. It never seems to strike anyone as a rum way of doing things.

The Queen loves muffins, so on her left she has a shiny chrome double-sided toaster into which she pops them from a pile on a plate, handed to her by her page. In the old days they used to toast them by the fire, but not any more. Even so, it's fair to say that toasting the muffins is the only cooking the Queen ever does.

By Royal Invitation (1988),
Unity Hall and Ingrid Seward

The National Anthem

ALL RIGHT, SO BEING ASKED to tea with the Queen is unlikely, but there is every chance that at some point in your life you will be expected to sing the national anthem. It has six verses. Usually only the first verse is sung, and very occasionally the first and third verses. The last line is sometimes sung as 'God save *the* Queen', rather than '*our* Queen'. The second verse is omitted due to its rather jingoistic tones, and the rest ... well, there is seldom time to keep Her Majesty waiting that long. Scouts and Guides are likely to know both the first and third verses. It is surprising how many younger members of the Royal Family do not.

1. God save our gracious Queen,
   Long live our noble Queen,
   God save the Queen!
   Send her victorious,
   Happy and glorious,
   Long to reign over us,
   God save our Queen!

2. O Lord our God arise,
    Scatter her enemies
    And make them fall;
    Confound their politics,
    Frustrate their knavish tricks,
    On thee our hopes we fix,
    God save us all!

3. Thy choicest gifts in store
    On her be pleased to pour;
    Long may she reign;
    May she defend our laws,
    And ever give us cause
    To sing with heart and voice,
    God save our Queen!

4. Not in this land alone,
    But be God's mercies known
    From shore to shore!
    Lord make the nations see,
    That men should brothers be,
    And form one family,
    The wide world o'er.

5. From every latent foe,
   From the assassin's blow,
   God save the Queen!
   O'er her thine arm extend,
   For Britain's sake defend
   Our mother, prince and friend,
   God save the Queen!

6. Lord Grant that Marshal Wade*
   May by thy mighty aid
   Victory bring.
   May he sedition hush,
   And like a torrent rush,
   Rebellious Scots to crush.
   God save the Queen!

* Field Marshal Wade, as commander of the English forces under King George II, had to deal with the Jacobite insurrection in 1745 and an attempted invasion of England by the Scots. At that time the anthem would have been 'God save the King'.

Titles

A ND IF YOU NEVER GET to meet the Queen, maybe you will at least get to meet a duke, or a knight, or an earl, or a baronet. But even they are not always treated with the respect that befits their station in life; take Sir Thomas Ingilby.

The English love titles. If you can't be an earl or viscount, 'community advisory officer' or 'customer services officer' seems to carry almost as much cachet. There is no doubt that our understanding of contemporary hierarchy is far better than our grasp of the hereditary system that we grew up with. I once hired a car at Jersey airport under a completely assumed name – by mistake. The girl behind the desk greeted me and then asked me to hand over my driving licence. I duly complied. She painstakingly wrote down the relevant details, then handed me the keys to an almost new Ford Escort. It wasn't until I checked the paperwork a day or two later that I realised I was driving around Jersey under the pseudonym Mr Sid Bart, a considerable but ingenious abbreviation of Sir Thomas Ingilby, Bt.

The Americans tend to go the other way. No matter how carefully or how many times I introduce myself, I always seem to end up being introduced to third parties as 'Lord Inglesby'. The Duke of Richmond and Gordon, then resident at Goodwood, recalls sitting down at an official banquet in the United States. The place to his right remained mysteriously vacant throughout the first course. It wasn't until he leaned across to read the place card and thus discover who hadn't turned up that he realised that his hosts had been expecting him to bring a friend. On his place card was written, 'the Duke of Richmond'. On the neighbouring place card it simply said, 'Gordon'.

> *Yorkshire's Great Houses* (2003),
> Sir Thomas Ingilby

The Orders of Chivalry and Ceremonial Offices

ORIGINALLY RESERVED FOR THE MONARCH and members of his family and his immediate aristocratic supporters, the orders of chivalry have been democratised over the last hundred years or so. The honours list is scrutinised by a committee of privy counsellors before being submitted to the sovereign. The most important orders are:

Order of the Garter

Instituted by King Edward III in 1348 and limited to the sovereign and twenty-four Knights Companion. Traditionally in the gift of the sovereign. The distinctive features are the Star, the Garter and the blue diagonal ribbon. The chapel of the order is at Windsor.

Order of the Thistle

Revived by King James VII in 1687 and re-founded by Queen Anne in 1703. It was originally established in the fifteenth century and is restricted to the sovereign and sixteen Scottish knights. The sash is a green ribbon.

Order of the Bath

Established by King George I in 1725. It has a civilian and a military division with three ranks in each class.

Order of Merit

Established by King Edward VII in 1902 and limited to twenty-four members. It is usually conferred upon those who have given exceptional service in their chosen field – especially in the arts and literature.

Order of the Companions of Honour

Established in 1917 by King George V and sometimes regarded as a junior class of the Order of Merit. Conferred upon men and women for services of national importance. Limited to the sovereign and sixty-five members, not including foreigners, who are admitted only as honorary members.

Order of St Michael and St George

Established in 1818, this order is reserved mainly for diplomats.

Royal Victorian Order

Founded by Queen Victoria in 1896 for members of the royal household and others who have given exceptional service.

Order of the British Empire

Established in 1917. There are five grades: Knight (or Dame) Grand Cross, Knight (or Dame) Commander, Commander, Officer and Member.

Lord Lieutenant

The representative of the Crown for each county in the United Kingdom. The Lord Lieutenant may be a peer or a commoner, male or female. Originally appointed as part of the reorganisation of local government in the reign of King Henry VIII to take over the military duties of the sheriff and control the military forces of the Crown. The Forces Act of 1871 transferred those powers back to the Crown. Today's Lord Lieutenant will be a distinguished person in the county and responsible for royal visits. A Lord Lieutenant will have one Vice Lord Lieutenant and a number of Deputy Lieutenants depending upon the size of the county. Lord Lieutenants are also responsible for recommending people for appointment as Justices of the Peace. The retiring age is seventy-five. Lord Lieutenants wear a military-style navy-blue uniform with a scarlet stripe down the trousers and a scarlet band round the hat. They may also carry a sword. The Deputy Lieutenants may be similarly attired but with a maroon sash rather than a sash of maroon and silver. Female Lord Lieutenants have no formal uniform.

High Sheriffs

The office has existed since before the Norman Conquest – at which time the holder was the official, or reeve, who looked after the royal demesne in the shire; hence 'shire-reeve' or 'sheriff'. Today the office is of only ceremonial importance, though the Sheriff is also called upon to act as the returning officer in the event of a general election and to announce the accession of a new sovereign. It is also his job to appoint an Under-Sheriff, who is responsible for enforcing certain High Court orders. The Sheriff of each county is selected each year by the sovereign, who 'pricks' the name of each successful nominee upon the roll of parchment presented to her by the Clerk of the Privy Council. For this the sovereign uses a bodkin – a tradition that dates back to Elizabeth I. The appointment lasts for one year, and the High Sheriff is likely to be called upon to officiate at everything from official ceremonies, dinners and royal visits to the presentation of prizes at school speech days, as well as looking after visiting members of the judiciary. The uniform consists of a black velvet jacket and knee breeches, silk hose, lace jabeau and cuffs, buckled shoes, a sword and a fore-and-aft hat which is carried rather than worn.

England
and St George

Once more unto the breach, dear friends, once more;
Or close the wall up with our English dead!
In peace there's nothing so becomes a man
As modest stillness and humility:
But when the blast of war blows in our ears,
Then imitate the action of the tiger;
Stiffen the sinews, conjure up the blood,
Disguise fair nature with hard-favoured rage;
Then lend the eye a terrible aspect;
Let it pry through the portage of the head
Like the brass cannon; let the brow o'erwhelm it
As fearfully as doth a gallèd rock
O'erhang and jutty his confounded base,
Swilled with the wild and wasteful ocean.
Now set the teeth, and stretch the nostril wide,
Hold hard the breath, and bend up every spirit
To his full height. On, on, you noblest English,
Whose blood is fet from fathers of war-proof!
Fathers that, like so many Alexanders,
Have in these parts from morn till even fought,
And sheathed their swords for lack of argument:
Dishonour not your mothers; now attest

England, Our England

That those whom you called father did beget you.
Be copy now to men of grosser blood,
And teach them how to war. And you, good yeomen,
Whose limbs were made in England, show us here
The mettle of your pasture; let us swear
That you are worth your breeding; which I doubt not;
For there is none of you so mean and base,
That hath not noble lustre in your eyes.
I see you stand like greyhounds in the slips,
Straining upon the start. The game's afoot:
Follow your spirit, and upon this charge
Cry, 'God for Harry, England, and Saint George!'

Henry V (1599), Act III, Scene 1,
William Shakespeare (1564–1616)

St George

THERE IS MUCH CONTROVERSY SURROUNDING St George, and his claim to be the patron saint of England. Some suggest he was not even English. *The Oxford Book of Saints* suggests that he was a soldier who died around 303 AD.

The story of St George and the dragon became popular in the West thanks to *The Golden Legend*, which was translated and printed by William Caxton. The dragon terrorised the whole of the country and could poison with its breath anyone who approached it. Every day it was appeased with an offering of two sheep, but eventually the sheep ran out and a human sacrifice had to be made. The lot fell upon the King's daughter, who was dressed as a bride and led to her fate. Enter St George, who pierced the dragon with his lance and led it away with the princess's girdle, telling the people that if they would believe in Jesus Christ they would have nothing to fear and the monster would be conquered. The King and the people agreed. George killed the dragon and 15,000 men were baptised. George asked for no reward, but that the King maintain churches, honour priests and look after the poor.

A vision of St George during the Siege of Antioch in the

Crusades did more to venerate his name and resulted in him becoming the patron saint of soldiers.

Edward III founded the Order of the Garter under his patronage in the fourteenth century, and St George's Chapel at Windsor is dedicated to him.

After the Battle of Agincourt, when Henry V's speech invoked St George as England's patron saint, his feast day was elevated in rank.

According to the poet Edmund Spenser:

> Thou, among those saints which thou dost see,
> Shalt be a saint and thine own nation's friend
> And patron; thou Saint George shalt called be,
> St George of merry England, the sign of victory.

The Faerie Queen (1596),
Edmund Spenser (*c.*1552–99)

St George's feast day is 23 April, but in the reform of the Roman calendar in 1969 'His cult was reduced to a local one.' Shame.

Main Saints' Days

THESE ARE THE MOST RECOGNISED saints' days, along with what are called 'fixed festivals', which occupy the same date each year.

JANUARY

1 Circumcision
6 Epiphany
25 Conversion of St Paul

FEBRUARY

2 Purification
14 St Valentine

MARCH

1 St David
17 St Patrick
19 St Joseph
25 Annunciation

April

23 St George
25 St Mark

May

3 St Philip and St James
14 St Matthias

June

11 St Barnabas
24 St John the Baptist
29 St Peter and St Paul

July

3 St Thomas
22 St Mary Magdalene
25 St James

August

6 Transfiguration
15 Assumption
24 St Bartholomew

September

8 Blessed Virgin Mary
21 St Matthew
29 St Michael

October

18 St Luke
28 St Simon and St Jude

November

1 All Saints
30 St Andrew

December

25 Christmas Day
26 St Stephen
27 St John the Evangelist
28 Holy Innocents

He is an Englishman!
For he himself has said it,
And it's greatly to his credit,
That he is an Englishman!
For he might have been a Roosian,
A French, or Turk, or Proosian,
Or perhaps Itali-an!
But in spite of all temptations,
To belong to other nations,
He remains an Englishman!
Hurrah!
For the true-born Englishman!

'The Englishman', *HMS Pinafore* (1878),
W. S. Gilbert (1836–1911)

King Arthur and the Knights of the Round Table

HOW MUCH IS LEGEND and how much is truth? There are so many opinions, and so many knights – around 150 of them all told – though some sources list as many as 366. They were noble men who fought for their king and country in the fifth or sixth century at King Arthur's court, Camelot.

The Round Table is in the Great Hall at Winchester, mounted on the wall for all to see, even though carbon-dating suggests it is not the original. It is said to have been devised by Merlin, a prophet and sorcerer who foresaw the quest for the Holy Grail and who saw the reign of King Arthur as one way of achieving a perfect world.

Arthur's queen was Guinevere, who fell from grace by falling in love and committing adultery with one of the knights – Sir Lancelot – causing the knights of the Round Table to split into two factions. Then there was Mordred, born as a result of incest between Arthur and his half-sister, Margawse. Mordred seized the kingdom during Arthur's absence.

Arthur is buried at Avalon – thought by some to be Glastonbury Tor.

The Knights

The main Knights of the Round Table are:

King Arthur

Sir Gawain

Sir Lancelot

Sir Percival

Sir Galahad

Sir Bors

Sir Kay

Sir Bedivere

Sir Girflet

Sir Yvain

Sir Erec

King Pellinor

Sir Tristan

Sir Morholt

Sir Dinadan

Palemedes (*a Saracen knight*)

Cador, Duke of Cornwall

Hoel, Duke of Brittany
Lucan the Butler (*brother of Sir Bedivere*)
Sir Agravain
Sir Gaheris
Sir Gareth
Mordred
Galeshin (*son of King Neutres of Garlot*)
Sir Yvain the Bastard
Sir Hector
Sir Lamerocke
Guinglain, the Fair Unknown (*son of Sir Gawain*)
King Baudemagus of Gorre
Sir Sagremor
Sir Lionel.

And the list goes on and on.

THIS IS A CHAPTER OF UNALLOYED patriotism, so we might just as well get on with it and haul out the usual suspects, and a few that are unexpected.

'Land of Hope and Glory'

'LAND OF HOPE AND GLORY', with Sir Edward Elgar's music and words by Arthur C. Benson, has become our second national anthem and is usually accompanied by much flag-waving, to the horror of those who deplore such demonstrations of national pride.

1. Dear Land of Hope, thy hope is crowned.
    God make thee mightier yet!
    On Sov'reign brows, beloved, renowned,
    Once more thy crown is set.
    Thine equal laws, by Freedom gained,
    Have ruled thee well and long;
    By Freedom gained, by Truth maintained,
    Thine Empire shall be strong.

    Chorus
    Land of Hope and Glory,
    Mother of the Free,
    How shall we extol thee,
    Who are born of thee?

Wider still and wider shall thy bounds be set;
God, who made thee mighty,
Make thee mightier yet;
God, who made thee mighty,
Make thee mightier yet.

2. Thy fame is ancient as the days,
As Ocean large and wide;
A pride that dares, and heeds not praise,
A stern and silent pride;
Not that false joy that dreams content
With what our sires have won;
The blood a hero sire hath spent
Still nerves a hero son.

Chorus

'Land of Hope and Glory' (1902),
Arthur C. Benson (1862–1925)

Jerusalem

BLAKE WROTE 'AND DID THOSE feet in ancient time' as a preface to his epic poem *Milton*. Sir Hubert Parry set the words to music in 1916. Blake was apparently inspired by the apocryphal story of the young Jesus visiting England in the company of Joseph of Arimathea. The Glastonbury thorn tree is said to have sprung from Joseph's staff. The words and music together have become a national anthem, sung with passion at the Last Night of the Proms along with 'Land of Hope and Glory'.

> And did those feet in ancient time
> Walk upon England's mountains green?
> And was the holy Lamb of God
> On England's pleasant pastures seen?
>
> And did the Countenance Divine
> Shine forth upon our clouded hills?
> And was Jerusalem builded here
> Among these dark Satanic mills?

Bring me my bow of burning gold;
Bring me my arrows of desire;
Bring me my spear; O clouds unfold!
Bring me my chariot of fire.

I will not cease from mental strife,*
Nor shall my sword sleep in my hand,
Till we have built Jerusalem,
In England's green and pleasant land.

'Jerusalem' (1804–1810),
William Blake (1757–1827)

* Later versions substitute 'fight' for Blake's original 'strife'.

'I Vow to Thee, My Country'

GUSTAV HOLST (1874–1934), English, in spite of his name, wrote the music to which the words by Sir Cecil Spring-Rice are sung. It is part of his *Planets* suite, representing Jupiter, 'the bringer of jollity', which makes it somewhat ironic that the hymn is often sung at funerals. Wherever you sing it, it has the power to get blood coursing through the veins. The music is majestic, and the words have a confident power.

I vow to thee, my country – all earthly things above –
Entire and whole and perfect, the service of my love,
The love that asks no question, the love that stands the test,
That lays upon the altar the dearest and the best,
The love that never falters, the love that pays the price,
The love that makes undaunted the final sacrifice.

And there's another country, I've heard of long ago,
Most dear to them that love her, most great to them that know;
We may not count her armies, we may not see her king;

England, Our England

Her fortress is a faithful heart, her pride is suffering;
And soul by soul and silently her shining bounds increase,
And her ways are ways of gentleness and all her paths are
   peace.

'I Vow to Thee, My Country' (1918),
Sir Cecil Spring-Rice (1859–1918)

B<small>UT LET'S BE HONEST ABOUT IT</small>. England is not perfect, as Charles Churchill recognised:

> Be England what she will,
> With all her faults, she is my country still.

The Farewell (1764),
Charles Churchill (1731–64)

William Cowper agreed:

> England, with all thy faults, I love thee still –
> My country! and, while yet a nook is left
> Where English minds and manners may be found,
> Shall be constrained to love thee. Tho' thy clime
> Be fickle, and thy year most part deformed
> With dripping rains, or withered by a frost,
> I would not yet exchange thy sullen skies,
> And fields without a flower, for warmer France
> With all her vines.

'The Timepiece' (1785),
William Cowper (1731–1800)

A ND NOËL COWARD WAS FORCED to admit that our opti-
mism is sometimes misplaced:

They're out of sorts in Sunderland
And terribly cross in Kent,
They're dull in Hull
And the Isle of Mull
Is seething with discontent,
They're nervous in Northumberland
And Devon is down the drain,
They're filled with wrath
On the Firth of Forth
And sullen on Salisbury Plain,
In Dublin they're depressed, lads,
Maybe because they're Celts
For Drake is going West, lads,
And so is everyone else.
Hurray! Hurray! Hurray!
Misery's here to stay.

There are bad times just around the corner,
There are dark clouds hurtling through the sky
And it's no good whining
About a silver lining

For we know from experience that they won't roll by,
With a scowl and a frown
We'll keep our peckers down
And prepare for depression and doom and dread,
We're going to unpack our troubles from our old kit bag
And wait until we drop down dead.

From Portland Bill to Scarborough
They're querulous and subdued
And Shropshire lads
Have behaved like cads
From Berwick-on-Tweed to Bude,
They're mad at Market Harborough
And livid at Leigh-on-Sea,
In Tunbridge Wells
You can hear the yells
Of woe-begone bourgeoisie.
We all get bitched about, lads,
Whoever our vote elects,
We know we're up the spout, lads,
And that's what England expects.
Hurray! Hurray! Hurray!
Trouble is on the way.

There are bad times just around the corner,
The horizon's gloomy as can be,

England, Our England

There are black birds over
The greyish cliffs of Dover
And the rats are preparing to leave the BBC.
We're an *un*happy breed
And very bored indeed
When reminded of something that Nelson said.
While the press and the politicians nag nag nag
We'll wait until we drop down dead.

From Colwyn Bay to Kettering
They're sobbing themselves to sleep,
The shrieks and wails
In the Yorkshire Dales
Have even depressed the sheep.
In rather vulgar lettering
A very disgruntled group
Have posted bills
On the Cotswold Hills
To prove that we're in the soup.
While begging Kipling's pardon
There's one thing we know for sure,
If England is a garden
We ought to have more manure.
Hurray! Hurray! Hurray!
Suffering and dismay.

England and St George

There are bad times just around the corner
And the outlook's absolutely vile,
There are Home Fires smoking
From Windermere to Woking
And we're *not* going to tighten our belts and smile smile smile,
At the sound of a shot
We'd just as soon as not
Take a hot-water bottle and go to bed,
We're going to *un*tense our muscles till they sag sag sag
And wait until we drop down dead.

There are bad times just around the corner,
We can all look forward to despair,
It's as clear as crystal
From Bridlington to Bristol
That we can't save democracy and we don't much care
If the Reds and the Pinks
Believe that England stinks
And that world revolution is bound to spread,
We'd better all learn the lyrics of the old 'Red Flag'
And wait until we drop down dead.
A likely story
Land of Hope and Glory,
Wait until we drop down dead.

'There are Bad Times Just Around the Corner' (1953),
Noël Coward (1899–1973)

53

B UT WITH ALL ITS SHORTCOMINGS, there really is no place like England, and it's time we let the rest of them know that as a people we are unbeatable:

The rottenest bits of these islands of ours
We've left in the hands of three unfriendly powers;
Examine the Irishman, Welshman or Scot,
You'll find he's a stinker as likely as not!

The English, the English, the English are best!
I wouldn't give tuppence for all of the rest!

The Scotsman is mean, as we're all well aware,
And bony and blotchy and covered with hair;
He eats salty porridge, he works all the day
And he hasn't got bishops to show him the way.

The English, the English, the English are best!
I wouldn't give tuppence for all of the rest!

The Irishman now our contempt is beneath;
He sleeps in his boots, and he lies in his teeth;
He hates all the English, or so I have heard,
And blames it on Cromwell and William the Third.

England and St George

The English are noble, the English are nice,
And worth any other at double the price!

The Welshman's dishonest – he cheats when he can –
And little and dark, more like monkey than man;
He works underground with a lamp in his hat
And sings far too loud, far too often, and flat.

The English, the English, the English are best!
I wouldn't give tuppence for all of the rest!

And crossing the Channel one cannot say much
For the French or the Spanish, the Danish or Dutch;
The Germans are German, the Russians are Red,
And the Greeks and Italians eat garlic in bed.

The English are moral, the English are good
And clever and modest and misunderstood.

And all the world over each nation's the same –
They've simply no notion of playing the game;
They argue with umpires, they cheer when they've won,
And they practise beforehand, which spoils all the fun!

The English, the English, the English are best!
So up with the English and down with the rest!

It's not that they're wicked or naturally bad:
It's knowing they're *foreign* that makes them so mad!
For the English are all that a nation should be,
And the flower of the English are you, dear reader, and me!

The English, the English, the English are best!
I wouldn't give tuppence for all of the rest!

'Song of Patriotic Prejudice' (1963),
Michael Flanders (1922–75) and Donald Swann (1923–94)

When We Were
Very Young

WE CANNOT SEE OURSELVES WHEN very young, but we can see our children, and see in them something of ourselves. I found this piece by Laurie Lee several years ago, and, as the father of daughters, its truths struck home.

I met Laurie Lee a number of times. He was a roguish, jowly, white-haired man with horn-rimmed glasses and a twinkle in his eye. His voice had a rich Gloucestershire burr. I think he recognised my admiration, though I tried not to be too effusive. He said that he listened to me on the radio on a Saturday morning, giving out my gardening advice. The programme went out at 7.50 a.m. each week, and he inscribed in my copy of *Cider With Rosie*: 'To Alan, the lucifer of the morning, with dazzled eyes, Laurie Lee.'

I am every bit as dazzled by this:

She was born in the autumn and was a late fall in my life, and lay purple and dented like a little bruised plum, as though she'd been lightly trodden in the grass and forgotten.

Then the nurse lifted her up and she came suddenly alive, her bent legs kicking crabwise, and her first living gesture was a thin wringing of the hands accompanied by a far-out Hebridean lament.

This moment of meeting seemed to be a birthtime for both of us; her first and my second life. Nothing, I knew, would be the same again, and I think I was reasonably shaken. I peered intently at her, looking for familiar signs, but she was convulsed as an Aztec idol. Was this really my daughter, this purple concentration of anguish, this blind and protesting dwarf?

Then they handed her to me, stiff and howling, and I held her for the first time and kissed her, and she went still and quiet as though by instinctive guile, and I was instantly enslaved by her flattery of my powers.

Only a few brief months have passed since that day, but already I've felt all the obvious astonishments. New-born, of course, she looked already a centenarian, tottering on the brink of an old crone's grave, exhausted, shrunken, bald as Voltaire, mopping, mowing, and twisting wrinkled claws in speechless spasms of querulous doom.

But with each day of survival she has grown younger and fatter, her face filling, drawing on life, every breath of real air healing the birth-death stain she had worn so witheringly at the beginning.

Now this girl, my child, this parcel of will and warmth, fills the cottage with her obsessive purpose. The rhythmic tides of her sleeping and feeding spaciously measure the days and nights. Her frail self-absorption is a commanding presence, her helplessness strong as a rock, so that I find myself listening even to her silences as though some great engine was purring upstairs.

When awake, and not feeding, she snorts and gobbles, dryly, like a ruminative jackdaw, or strains and groans and waves her hands about as though casting invisible nets.

When I watch her at this I see her hauling in life, groping fiercely with every limb and muscle, working blind at a task no one can properly share, in a darkness where she is still alone.

She is of course just an ordinary miracle, but is also the particular late wonder of my life. So each night I take her to bed like a book and lie close and study her. Her dark blue eyes stare straight into mine, but off-centre, not seeing me.

Such moments could be the best we shall ever know – those midnights of mutual blindness. Already, I suppose, I should be afraid for her future, but I am more concerned with mine.

I am fearing perhaps her first acute recognition, her first questions, the first man she makes of me. But for the moment I'm safe: she stares idly through me, at the pillow, at the light on the wall, and each is a shadow of purely nominal value and she prefers neither one to the other.

Meanwhile as I study her I find her early strangeness insidiously claiming a family face.

Here she is then, my daughter, here, alive, the one I must possess and guard. A year ago this space was empty, not even a hope of her was in it. Now she's here, brand new, with our name upon her; and no one will call in the night to reclaim her.

She is here for good, her life stretching before us, twenty-odd years wrapped up in that bundle; she will grow, learn to totter, to run in the garden, run back, and call this place home. Or will she?

Looking at those weaving hands and complicated ears, the fit of the skin round that delicate body, I can't indulge in the neurosis of imagining all this to be merely a receptacle for Strontium 90. The forces within her seem much too powerful to submit to a blanket death of that kind.

But she could, even so, be a victim of chance; all those quick lively tendrils seem so vulnerable to their own recklessness – surely she'll fall on the fire, or roll down some crevice, or kick herself out of the window?

I realise I'm succumbing to the occupational disease, the father-jitters or new-parenthood-shakes, expressed in, 'Hark, the child's screaming, she must be dying.' Or, 'She's so quiet, she must be dead.'

As it is, my daughter is so new to me still that I can't yet leave her alone. I have to keep on digging her out of her sleep to make sure that she's really alive.

She is a time-killing lump, her face a sheaf of masks which she shuffles through aimlessly. One by one she reveals them, while I watch eerie rehearsals of those emotions she will one day need; random, out-of-sequence but already exact, automatic but strangely knowing – a quick pucker of fury, a puff of ho-hum boredom, a beaming after-dinner smile, perplexity, slyness, a sudden wrinkling of grief, pop-eyed interest and fat-lipped love.

It is more than a month since I was handed this living heap of expectations, and I can feel nothing but simple awe.

What have I got exactly? And what am I going to do with her? And what for that matter will she do with me?

I have got a daughter, whose life is already separate from mine, whose will already follows its own directions, and who has quickly corrected my woolly preconceptions of her by being something remorselessly different. She is the child of herself and will be what she is. I am merely the keeper of her temporary helplessness.

Even so, with luck, she can alter me; indeed, is doing so now. At this stage in my life she will give me more than she gets, and may even later become *my* keeper.

But if I could teach her anything at all – by unloading upon her some of the ill-tied parcels of my years – I'd like it to be acceptance and a holy relish for life. To accept with gladness the fact of being a woman – when she'll find all nature to be on her side.

If pretty, to thank God and enjoy her luck and not start beefing about being loved for her mind. To be willing to give pleasure without feeling loss of face, to prefer charm to the vanity of aggression, and not to deliver her powers and mysteries into the opposite camp by wishing to compete with men.

In this way, I believe – though some of her sisters may disapprove – she might know some happiness and also spread some around.

And as a brief tenant of this precious and irreplaceable world, I'd ask her to preserve life both in herself and others. To prefer always Societies for Propagation and Promotion rather than those for the Abolition or Prevention of.

Never to persecute others for the sins hidden in herself, nor to seek justice in terms of vengeance; to avoid like a plague all acts of mob-righteousness; to take cover whenever flags start flying; and to accept her faults and frustrations as her own personal burden, and not to blame them too often, if she can possibly help it, on young or old, whites or coloureds, East, West, Jews, Gentiles, television, bingo, trades unions, the City, school-milk or the British Railways.

For the rest, she may be my own salvation, for any man's child is his second chance. In this role I see her leading me back to my beginnings, reopening rooms I'd locked and forgotten, stirring the dust in my mind by re-asking the big questions – as any child can do.

But in my case, perhaps, just not too late; she persuades me there may yet be time, that with her, my tardy but bright-eyed pathfinder, I may return to that wood which long ago I fled from, but which together we may now enter and know.

The Firstborn (1964),
Laurie Lee (1914–97)

A N ENGLISH CHILDHOOD IS for most of us a mixed bag.
There are moments of high anxiety and a feeling of not
fitting in, and others of pure and innocent bliss.

I grew up in the Yorkshire Dales, where the scenery and the
opportunities for 'playing out' during a childhood in the
1950s and 1960s were taken full advantage of. My surroundings were enviable – woods filled with bluebells, the moors
with their heather, bracken and grouse, and the river with its
fish and endless opportunities for make-believe.

But there were still the agonies – the occasional loneliness
of being on the fringes of childhood society. I had a good re-
lationship with my parents for the most part, but Alan Bennett, who grew up fifteen miles away from where I did, and
who is fifteen years older than I am, seemed rather more uncomfortable with his.

As a child I am always conscious – and always guilty – that
I love my mother more than my father. I am happier with her
than with him, feel easier alone in her company, whereas
with him I am awkward and over-talkative and not the kind
of boy (modest, unassuming, unpretentious) that I feel he
wants me to be and has been himself.

In my teens I became fearful that my mother and, to a
lesser extent, my father will die. My concern is not entirely

unselfish – 'What will happen to me?' is probably at the bottom of it – and it declares itself in an odd fashion.

Both my parents have false teeth. Dad has all his teeth out when he is twenty-five, and having been a martyr to toothache for much of his youth he counts himself well rid of them. With Mam it takes longer but eventually she has all hers out too. This is not unusual at the time, having your teeth out being almost a rite of passage before entering middle-age.

So when I am fourteen or so, both my parents have long had false teeth (and called that, never dentures). At night Dad sleeps in his top set but takes out his bottom teeth and leaves them on the draining board. Mam, who is that much more hygienic, puts her set in a glass, or, more often, a cup that has lost its handle. They will have given them a perfunctory going-over with an ancient brush, but the teeth are never immersed in any cleanser other than water so they are always coated in a greyish lichen-like fur that is very hard to brush off, with Dad's teeth noticeably worse than Mam's as he is still in those days a smoker.

At fourteen I am convinced that this coating is a bad thing and that it harbours every known germ, and that my parents' health and indeed survival depends on it being removed. So, every night after they have gone to bed, I take it upon myself to scrub and swill their teeth to try and rid the plates of this grey accretion, noting even then that the proportion of dentures I have to do, two for Mam and one for

Dad, corresponds fittingly with the respective degree of affection I bear, or think I bear, for each of them.

That I undertake this nightly ritual cleansing is never acknowledged by them or referred to by me, but it must seem odd, particularly to my father. What is this strange creature they have nurtured ... still at fourteen looking like a boy of ten, never away from church or the library, and given to furtively scrubbing their false teeth? It's no wonder that Dad seems to have little time for me or that there are none of the conventional rows he's had with my brother at the same age and who is already asserting his independence in the stock ways, smoking on the quiet, coming home tipsy once or twice – stages in adolescence Dad has long been led to expect. But who has ever heard of a son who scrubs his parents' false teeth? The best plan is to say nothing and hope that it will pass.

My father is a butcher, working until he's forty for the Leeds Co-op and then branching out on his own in a succession of small shops which make us a living but not much more. He doesn't look like a butcher, should never have been one, my mother says, and would have been happier as a violinist.

Telling Tales (2000),
Alan Bennett (1934–)

Beatrix Potter
(1866–1943)

OTHER CHILDREN GREW UP with A. A. Milne and *Winnie the Pooh*; I think my parents must have thought Pooh too posh. Beatrix Potter's tales, though, were classless. She was also a woman of the Lakes – just above Yorkshire, where we would go on daytrips to see Windermere and Ullswater, so that must have made her seem even more like one of us.

The Tale of Peter Rabbit remains my favourite, in spite of the fact that it introduced me to the grumpy gardener, Mr Mc-Gregor (which, surprisingly, did not put me off the trade). It also mentions 'bread and milk and blackberries', which sounded very comforting – unlike the camomile tea, which did not. But not all Beatrix Potter's books were cosy. I remember being unsettled by *The Tale of Squirrel Nutkin*, and yet never being able to put my finger on exactly why.

The Complete Works

The Tale of Peter Rabbit – 1901 (privately printed)
The Tale of Peter Rabbit – 1902
The Tailor of Gloucester – 1902 (privately printed)
The Tale of Squirrel Nutkin – 1903
The Tailor of Gloucester – 1903
The Tale of Benjamin Bunny – 1904
The Tale of Two Bad Mice – 1904
The Tale of Mrs Tiggy-Winkle – 1905
The Tale of the Pie and the Patty-Pan – 1905
The Tale of Mr Jeremy Fisher – 1906
The Story of a Fierce Bad Rabbit – 1906
The Story of Miss Moppet – 1906
The Tale of Tom Kitten – 1907
The Tale of Jemima Puddle-Duck – 1908
The Roly-Poly Pudding (later renamed *The Tale of Samuel Whiskers*)
   – 1908
The Tale of the Flopsy Bunnies – 1909
The Tale of Ginger and Pickles – 1909
The Tale of Mrs Tittlemouse – 1910
Peter Rabbit's Painting Book – 1911
The Tale of Timmy Tiptoes – 1911
The Tale of Mr Tod – 1912
The Tale of Pigling Bland – 1913
Tom Kitten's Painting Book – 1917

Appley Dapply's Nursery Rhymes – 1917
The Tale of Johnny Town-Mouse – 1918
Cecily Parsley's Nursery Rhymes – 1922
Jemima Puddle-Duck's Painting Book – 1925
Peter Rabbit's Almanac for 1929 – 1928
The Fairy Caravan – 1929
The Tale of Little Pig Robinson – 1930
Sister Anne (with illustrations by Katharine Sturges) – 1932
Wag-by-Wall – 1944

The last book was published posthumously, but then, as Margaret Lane remarked:

In Beatrix Potter's middle and old age not many people knew anything about her. Her name, of course, conjured up enchanting childhood memories of Peter Rabbit, Tom Kitten, Jemima Puddle-Duck and the rest, but it was generally assumed that she had long been dead.

On the other hand, there was another person, a Mrs William Heelis, wife of a solicitor in the Lake District, a woman well known locally as a farmer and shrewd purchaser of land, who could be bluntly outspoken at cattle shows and sheep fairs, and who pottered about in her own fields with a stout stick and usually, in wet and windy weather, a meal-sack across her shoulders. It was a fact known to remarkably few people that Beatrix Potter and Mrs Heelis were one and the same.

This was precisely as she would have wished. She had lived her life through three very different phases, and her sense of personal privacy was extreme. Her childhood cannot be described as happy. Lonely, restricted, in the stuffy and frustrating atmosphere of a prosperous middle-class household in which almost any form of activity was frowned upon, she consoled herself with the company of small animals, chiefly mice and rabbits, which she loved and studied with the absorbing passion of both naturalist and artist. 'I cannot rest,' she wrote in the secret-code journal which she kept from her fourteenth to her thirtieth year, 'I *must* draw, however poor the result ... I *will* do something sooner or later.'

The Tale of *Beatrix Potter* (2001),
Margaret Lane

If you can keep your head when all about you
    Are losing theirs and blaming it on you,
If you can trust yourself when all men doubt you,
    But make allowance for their doubting too;
If you can wait and not be tired by waiting,
    Or being lied about, don't deal in lies,
Or being hated, don't give way to hating,
    And yet don't look too good, nor talk too wise:

If you can dream – and not make dreams your master;
    If you can think – and not make thoughts your aim;
If you can meet with Triumph and Disaster
    And treat those two impostors just the same;
If you can bear to hear the truth you've spoken
    Twisted by knaves to make a trap for fools,
Or watch the things you gave your life to, broken,
    And stoop and build 'em up with worn-out tools:

If you can make one heap of all your winnings
    And risk it on one turn of pitch-and-toss,
And lose, and start again at your beginnings
    And never breathe a word about your loss;

When We Were Very Young

If you can force your heart and nerve and sinew
 To serve your turn long after they are gone,
And so hold on when there is nothing in you
 Except the Will which says to them: 'Hold on!'

If you can talk with crowds and keep your virtue,
 Or walk with Kings – nor lose the common touch,
If neither foes nor loving friends can hurt you,
 If all men count with you, but none too much;
If you can fill the unforgiving minute
 With sixty seconds' worth of distance run,
Yours is the Earth and everything that's in it,
 And – which is more – you'll be a Man, my son!

'If—' (1910),
Rudyard Kipling (1865–1936)

M Y SCHOOLDAYS WERE NOT THE happiest of my life; but then neither were those of Winston Churchill and he went to Harrow – not Ilkley Secondary Modern. I doubt that I would have enjoyed Latin, though it might have been useful when it came to learning and understanding plant names.

To Winston Churchill, though, it remained a mystery:

The school my parents had selected for my education was one of the most fashionable and expensive in the country . . .

When the last sound of my mother's departing wheels had died away, the headmaster invited me to hand over any money I had in my possession. I produced my three half-crowns, which were duly entered in a book, and I was told that from time to time there would be a 'shop' at the school with all sorts of things which one would like to have, and that I could choose what I liked up to the limit of the seven and sixpence. Then we quitted the headmaster's parlour and the comfortable private side of the house, and entered the more bleak apartments reserved for the instruction and accommodation of the pupils. I was taken into a form room and told to sit at a desk. All the other boys were out of doors, and I was alone with the form master. He produced a thin greeny-brown-covered book filled with words in different types of print.

'You have never done any Latin before, have you?' he said.

'No, sir.'

'This is a Latin grammar.' He opened it at a well-thumbed page. 'You must learn this,' he said, pointing to a number of words in a frame of lines. 'I will come back in half an hour and see what you know.'

Behold me then on a gloomy evening, with an aching heart, seated in front of the first declension.

mensa	a table
mensa	O table
mensam	a table
mensae	of a table
mensae	to or for a table
mensa	by, with or from a table

What on earth did it mean? Where was the sense in it? It seemed absolute rigmarole to me. However, there was one thing I could always do: I could learn by heart. And I thereupon proceeded, as far as my private sorrows would allow, to memorise the acrostic-looking task which had been set me.

In due course the master returned.

'Have you learnt it?' he asked.

'I think I can *say* it, sir,' I replied; and I gabbled it off.

He seemed so satisfied with this that I was emboldened to ask a question.

'What does it mean, sir?'

'It means what it says. *Mensa*, "a table". *Mensa* is a noun of the first declension. There are five declensions. You have learnt the singular of the first declension.'

'But,' I repeated, 'what does it mean?'

'*Mensa* means "a table",' he answered.

'Then why does *mensa* also mean "O table",' I enquired, 'and what does "O table" mean?'

'*Mensa*, "O table", is the vocative case,' he replied.

'But why "O table"?' I persisted in genuine curiosity.

' "O table" – you would use that in addressing a table, in invoking a table.' And then seeing he was not carrying me with him, 'You would use it in speaking to a table.'

'But I never do,' I blurted out in honest amazement.

'If you are impertinent, you will be punished, and punished, let me tell you, very severely,' was his conclusive rejoinder.

Such was my first introduction to the classics from which, I have been told, many of our cleverest men have derived so much solace and profit.

Winston S. Churchill (1874–1965),
Winston S. Churchill, *Selections from his Writings
and Speeches* (1952), ed. Guy Boas

Perhaps Churchill's tutor would have done better to concentrate on the English language, of which our future Prime Minister became a master. He'd have enjoyed this rhyme, now seldom quoted, which was written by the Lakeland poet Robert Southey at Keswick in 1820. It concerns the then famous Lodore Falls, which tumble from the fellside, and was described as a 'Rhyme for the nursery' and published in 1823 in Joanna Baillie's *A Collection of Poems, Chiefly Manuscript*. For all those who look at the waterfall today and exclaim, 'That's nice,' it might act as an object lesson on broadening the vocabulary. Long? Yes. Impressive? I think so.

'How does the water
Come down at Lodore?'
My little boy ask'd me
Thus, once on a time;
And moreover he task'd me
To tell him in rhyme.
Anon at the word,
There first came one daughter
And then came another,
To second and third
The request of their brother,
And to hear how the water

Comes down at Lodore,
With its rush and its roar,
As many a time
They had seen it before.
So I told them in rhyme,
For of rhymes I had store:
And 'twas in my vocation
For their recreation
That so I should sing;
Because I was Laureate
To them and the King.

From its sources which well
In the Tarn on the fell;
From its fountains
In the mountains,
Its rills and its gills;
Through moss and through brake,
It runs and it creeps
For awhile, till it sleeps
In its own little Lake.
And thence at departing,
Awakening and starting,
It runs through the reeds
And away it proceeds,

Through meadow and glade,
 In sun and in shade,
And through the wood-shelter,
 Among crags in its flurry,
  Helter-skelter,
  Hurry-scurry.
 Here it comes sparkling,
 And there it lies darkling;
Now smoking and frothing
 Its tumult and wrath in,
  Till in this rapid race
  On which it is bent,
  It reaches the place
  Of its steep descent.

 The Cataract strong
 Then plunges along,
 Striking and raging
  As if a war waging
Its caverns and rocks among:
  Rising and leaping,
  Sinking and creeping,
 Swelling and sweeping,
Showering and springing,
  Flying and flinging,
  Writhing and ringing,

Eddying and whisking,
   Spouting and frisking,
   Turning and twisting,
     Around and around
With endless rebound!
    Smiting and fighting
    A sight to delight in;
Confounding, astounding,
Dizzying and deafening the ear with its sound.

    Collecting, projecting,
    Receding and speeding,
    And shocking and rocking,
    And darting and parting,
    And threading and spreading,
    And whizzing and hissing,
    And dripping and skipping,
    And hitting and splitting,
    And shining and twining,
    And rattling and battling,
    And shaking and quaking,
    And pouring and roaring,
    And waving and raving,
    And tossing and crossing,
    And flowing and going,
    And running and stunning,

And foaming and roaming,
And dinning and spinning,
And dropping and hopping,
And working and jerking,
And guggling and struggling,
And heaving and cleaving,
And moaning and groaning;

And glittering and frittering,
And gathering and feathering,
And whitening and brightening,
And quivering and shivering,
And hurrying and scurrying,
And thundering and floundering;
Dividing and gliding and sliding,
And falling and brawling and sprawling,
And driving and riving and striving,
And sprinkling and twinkling and wrinkling,
And sounding and bounding and rounding,
And bubbling and troubling and doubling,
And grumbling and rumbling and tumbling,
And clattering and battering and shattering;

Retreating and beating and meeting and sheeting,
Delaying and straying and playing and spraying,
Advancing and prancing and glancing and dancing,

Recoiling, turmoiling and toiling and boiling,
And gleaming and streaming and steaming and beaming,
And rushing and flushing and brushing and gushing,
And flapping and rapping and clapping and slapping,
And curling and whirling and purling and twirling,
And thumping and plumping and bumping and jumping,
And dashing and flashing and splashing and clashing;
And so never ending, but always descending,
Sounds and motions for ever and ever are blending,
All at once and all o'er, with a mighty uproar,
And this way the water comes down at Lodore.

'The Cataract of Lodore' (1823),
Robert Southey (1774–1843)

When We Were Very Young

THE CHILDREN WHO DID LATIN were those who went to the grammar school, or those smaller, private schools up the posh end of town. You'd see them (and hear them) sometimes at the tennis club or the local gymkhana. That was when they really came into their own, their voices carrying like trumpets across the horseshoe-patterned turf.

It's awf'lly bad luck on Diana,
    Her ponies have swallowed their bits;
She fished down their throats with a spanner
    And frightened them all into fits.

So now she's attempting to borrow.
    Do lend her some bits, Mummy, *do*;
I'll lend her my own for tomorrow,
    But today *I*'ll be wanting them too.

Just look at Prunella on Guzzle,
    The wizardest pony on earth;
Why doesn't she slacken his muzzle,
    And tighten the breech in his girth?

I say, Mummy, there's Mrs Geyser
    And doesn't she look pretty sick?

I bet it's because Mona Lisa
 Was hit on the hock with a brick.

Miss Blewitt says Monica threw it,
 But Monica says it was Joan,
And Joan's very thick with Miss Blewitt,
 So Monica's sulking alone.

And Margaret failed in her paces,
 Her withers got tied in a noose,
So her coronets caught in the traces
 And now all her fetlocks are loose.

Oh, it's me now. I'm terribly nervous.
 I wonder if Smudges will shy.
She's practically certain to swerve as
 Her pelham is over one eye.

*

Oh, wasn't it naughty of Smudges?
 Oh, Mummy, I'm sick with disgust.
She threw me in front of the judges,
 And my silly old collarbone's bust.

'Hunter Trials' (1954),
Sir John Betjeman (1906–84)

Favourite English Children's Books

SOME OF THESE ARE VERY OLD, and some are very new.

Peepo! – Allan and Janet Ahlberg
The Oxford Nursery Rhyme Book – Iona and Peter Opie
the *Angelina Ballerina* series – Katharine Holabird (*illustrated by Helen Craig*)
Please, Mrs Butler – Allan Ahlberg (*illustrated by F. Wegner*)
the *Winnie the Pooh* series – A. A. Milne
When We Were Very Young – A. A. Milne (*illustrated by E. H. Shepard*)
the *Tales* series – Beatrix Potter
The Wind in the Willows – Kenneth Grahame
The Secret Seven series – Enid Blyton
The Famous Five series – Enid Blyton
the *Mallory Towers* series – Enid Blyton
the *Trebizon* series – Anne Digby
His Dark Materials – Philip Pullman
Swallows and Amazons – Arthur Ransome
the *Harry Potter* series – J. K. Rowling
The Chronicles of Narnia – C. S. Lewis

Peter Pan – J. M. Barrie

Treasure Island – Robert Louis Stevenson

Ballet Shoes – Noel Streatfeild

White Boots – Noel Streatfeild

Curtain Up – Noel Streatfeild

Black Beauty – Anna Sewell

The Borrowers series – Mary Norton

Lorna Doone – R. D. Blackmore

The Rattle Bag – edited by Seamus Heaney and Ted Hughes

Silver Snaffles – Primrose Cumming

Tales From the End Cottage – Eileen Bell

Stig of the Dump – Clive King

Alice in Wonderland – Lewis Carroll

The BFG – Roald Dahl (*illustrated by Quentin Blake*)

the *Tracy Beaker* series – Jacqueline Wilson

(Several of these authors are Scottish, but they write in English. Mostly.)

The Wind in the Willows

M Y FAVOURITE CHILDREN'S BOOK of all time remains *The Wind in the Willows*. For a country lad, it was a great escape, and over the years its appeal has, if anything, increased. Who could possibly be unaffected by the charms of the Mole and the Rat? I think I want to *live* in *The Wind in the Willows*.

It all seemed too good to be true. Hither and thither through the meadows he rambled busily, along the hedgerows, across the copses, finding everywhere birds building, flowers budding, leaves thrusting – everything happy, and progressive, and occupied. And instead of having an uneasy conscience pricking him and whispering 'Whitewash!' he somehow could only feel how jolly it was to be the only idle dog among all these busy citizens. After all, the best part of a holiday is perhaps not so much to be resting yourself, as to see all the other fellows busy working.

He thought his happiness was complete when, as he meandered aimlessly along, suddenly he stood by the edge of a full-fed river. Never in his life had he seen a river before –

this sleek, sinuous, full-bodied animal, chasing and chuckling, gripping things with a gurgle and leaving them with a laugh, to fling itself on fresh playmates that shook themselves free, and were caught and held again. All was a-shake and a-shiver — glints and gleams and sparkles, rustle and swirl, chatter and bubble. The Mole was bewitched, entranced, fascinated. By the side of the river he trotted as one trots, when very small, by the side of a man, who holds one spellbound by exciting stories; and when tired at last, he sat on the bank, while the river still chattered on to him, a babbling procession of the best stories in the world, sent from the heart of the earth to be told at last to the insatiable sea.

As he sat on the grass and looked across the river, a dark hole in the bank opposite, just above the water's edge, caught his eye, and dreamily he fell to considering what a nice snug dwelling-place it would make for an animal with few wants and fond of a bijou riverside residence, above flood level and remote from noise and dust. As he gazed, something bright and small seemed to twinkle down in the heart of it, vanished, then twinkled once more like a tiny star. But it could hardly be a star in such an unlikely situation; and it was too glittering and small for a glow-worm. Then, as he looked, it winked at him, and so declared itself to be an eye; and a small face began gradually to grow up round it, like a frame round a picture.

A brown little face, with whiskers.

A grave round face, with the same twinkle in its eye that had first attracted his notice.

Small neat ears and thick silky hair.

It was the Water Rat!

Then the two animals stood and regarded each other cautiously.

'Hullo, Mole!' said the Water Rat.

'Hullo, Rat!' said the Mole.

'Would you like to come over?' enquired the Rat presently.

'Oh, it's all very well to *talk*,' said the Mole, rather pettishly, he being new to a river and riverside life and its ways.

The Rat said nothing, but stooped and unfastened a rope and hauled on it; then lightly stepped into a little boat which the Mole had not observed. It was painted blue outside and white within, and was just the size for two animals; and the Mole's whole heart went out to it at once, even though he did not yet fully understand its uses.

The Rat sculled smartly across and made fast. Then he held up his fore-paw as the Mole stepped gingerly down. 'Lean on that!' he said. 'Now then, step lively!' and the Mole to his surprise and rapture found himself actually seated in the stern of a real boat.

'This has been a wonderful day!' said he, as the Rat shoved off and took to the sculls again. 'Do you know, I've never been in a boat before in all my life.'

'What?' cried the Rat, open-mouthed. 'Never been in a—you never—well, I—what have you been doing, then?'

'Is it so nice as all that?' asked the Mole shyly, though he was quite prepared to believe it as he leant back in his seat and surveyed the cushions, the oars, the rowlocks, and all the fascinating fittings, and he felt the boat sway lightly under him.

'Nice? It's the *only* thing,' said the Water Rat solemnly, as he leant forward for his stroke. 'Believe me, my young friend, there is *nothing* – absolutely nothing – half so much worth doing as simply messing about in boats. Simply messing,' he went on dreamily: 'messing – about – in – boats; messing—'

'Look ahead, Rat!' cried the Mole suddenly.

It was too late. The boat struck the bank full tilt. The dreamer, the joyous oarsman, lay on his back at the bottom of the boat, his heels in the air.

'– about in boats – or *with* boats,' the Rat went on composedly, picking himself up with a pleasant laugh. 'In or out of 'em, it doesn't matter. Nothing seems really to matter, that's the charm of it. Whether you get away, or whether you don't; whether you arrive at your destination or whether you reach somewhere else, or whether you never get anywhere at all, you're always busy, and you never do anything in particular; and when you've done it there's always something else to do, and you can do it if you like, but you'd much better not. Look here! If you've really nothing else on hand this morning, supposing we drop down the river together, and have a long day of it?'

The Mole waggled his toes from sheer happiness, spread his chest with a sigh of full contentment, and leant back blissfully into the soft cushions. '*What* a day I'm having!' he said. 'Let us start at once!'

The Wind in the Willows (1908),
Kenneth Grahame (1859–1932)

Swallows and Amazons

*S*wallows and Amazons exerted the same sort of charm on some of my friends – especially those who were keen on boats. These were the days when children's imaginations were well developed, when entertainment was home-made, not at the end of a piece of cable, and when it was possible for a little girl to be called Titty without fear of a snigger. Heigh-ho.

Captain John and the mate were getting together the really important stores and deciding what they could do without. The list had grown very much last night after supper. Roger was kept busy running up and down to the boathouse with all sorts of things that everybody agreed could not be left behind.

The mate's chief task was fitting out the galley, with the help of Mrs Jackson, the farmer's wife, who was lending the things.

'You'll want a kettle first and foremost,' said Mrs Jackson.

'And a saucepan and a frying-pan,' said mate Susan, looking at her list. 'I'm best at buttered eggs.'

'And are you really?' said Mrs Jackson. 'Most folk are best at boiled.'

'Oh, well, I don't count boiled,' said Susan.

Then there were the knives and forks and plates and mugs and spoons to be thought of, and biscuit tins, big ones to keep the food in, and smaller tins for tea and salt and sugar.

'We'll want rather a big one for sugar, won't we?' said Roger, who had come in and was waiting for something else to carry down to the boathouse.

'You won't bake, I don't suppose,' said Mrs Jackson.

'I think not,' said Mate Susan.

The pile of things on the kitchen table grew and grew as Susan crossed off the items on her list.

John and Titty came in to show her the new flag and to see how she was getting on.

'Who is going to be doctor?' she asked.

'Surgeon,' said Titty. 'It's always surgeon on board ship.'

'You are,' said John. 'You're the mate. It's the mate's job. He comes dancing on to the scene, "And well," says he, "and how are your arms and legs and liver and lungs and bones afeeling now?" Don't you remember?'

'Then I ought to take some bandages and medicines and things.'

'Oh, no,' said Titty. 'On desert islands they cure everything with herbs. We'll have all sorts of diseases, plagues, and fevers and things that no medicine is any good for and we'll cure them with herbs that the natives show us.'

At this point mother came in and settled the question. 'No

medicines,' she said. 'Anyone who wants doctoring is invalided home.'

'If it's really serious,' said Titty, 'but we can have a plague or a fever or two by ourselves.'

John said: 'What about a chart?'

Titty said that as the ocean had never been explored, there could not be any charts.

'But all the most exciting charts and maps have places on them that are marked "Unexplored".'

'Well, they won't be much good for those places,' said Titty.

'We ought to have a chart of some kind,' said John. 'It'll probably be all wrong, and it won't have the right names. We'll make our own names, of course.'

They found a good map that showed the lake in a local guidebook. Titty said it wasn't really a chart. John said it

would do. And Mrs Jackson said they could take it, but must keep it as dry as they could. That meant another tin box for things that had to be kept dry. They put in besides the guidebook some exercise books for logs and some paper for letters home. They also put in the ship's library. Titty had found on the shelves in the parlour a German Dictionary left by some former visitor. 'It's full of foreign language,' she said, 'and we shall want it for talking with the natives.' In the end it was left behind, because it was large and heavy, and also it might be the wrong language. Instead, Titty took *Robinson Crusoe*. 'It tells you what to do on an island,' she said. John took *The Seaman's Handybook*, and Part Three of *The Baltic Pilot*. Both books had belonged to his father, but John took them with him even on holidays. Mate Susan took *Simple Cooking for Small Households*.

At last, when almost everything was piled into the boathouse, just before it was time for Roger and Titty to go to bed, the whole crew went up the path into the pinewood to the Peak of Darien to look once more at the island. The sun was sinking over the western hills. There was a dead calm. Far away they saw the island and the still lake without a ripple on it, stretching away into the distance.

'I can't believe we're going to land on it,' said Titty.

'We aren't unless there's wind tomorrow,' said Captain John. 'We'll have to whistle for a wind.'

Titty and Roger, by agreement, whistled one tune after

another all the way home. As they came to the farm the leaves of the beech trees shivered overhead.

'You see,' said Titty, 'we've got some wind. Wake up early and we'll go out and do some more whistling before breakfast.'

Swallows and Amazons (1930),
Arthur Ransome (1884–1967)

Oh, to Be in England

SOME SECTIONS OF THIS BOOK are more lyrical than others by way of their subject matter. This one is especially rhapsodic for two reasons. The first is that I am passionate about the English countryside and our need to cherish it and to celebrate it. The words 'husbandry' and 'stewardship' are used all too seldom nowadays.

The second is that some of our finest and most emotive writing has been inspired by nature and the English landscape.

Oh, to be in England
Now that April's there,
And whoever wakes in England
Sees, some morning, unaware,
That the lowest boughs and the brushwood sheaf
Round the elm-tree bole are in tiny leaf,
While the chaffinch sings on the orchard bough
In England – now!

And after April, when May follows,
And the whitethroat builds, and all the swallows –
Hark! where my blossomed pear-tree in the hedge

Leans to the field and scatters on the clover
Blossoms and dewdrops – at the bent spray's edge –
That's the wise thrush; he sings each song twice over,
Lest you should think he never could recapture
The first fine careless rapture!
And though the fields look rough with hoary dew,
All will be gay when noontide wakes anew
The buttercups, the little children's dower,
– Far brighter than this gaudy melon-flower!

'Home-Thoughts from Abroad' (1845),
Robert Browning (1812–89)

English Counties

A H, NOW HERE'S A CONUNDRUM. How many are there? And whatever happened to Cumberland and Westmorland (with no 'e' in the middle, please), which, along with a few bits of Lancashire and Yorkshire, are now referred to as Cumbria? At least that ghastly thing Avon seems to have gone and left Bristol out on a limb, but Huntingdonshire has been swallowed up by Cambridgeshire. Rutland has come back though and the Isle of Wight has been given county status, so there is some justice.

Ah, well, here they all are, along with their populations, and I've tacked on those amorphous lumps that account for cities and urban sprawls that have now gained their own identity.

County	County Town*	Population (2005)
Bedfordshire	Bedford	582,600
Berkshire	Reading	812,200
Bristol*		398,300
Buckinghamshire	Aylesbury	700,100
Cambridgeshire	Cambridge	748,600
Cheshire	Chester	993,200
City of London	Westminster	9,200
Cornwall	Truro	519,400
County Durham	Durham	875,700
Cumbria	Carlisle	498,800
Derbyshire	Derby	981,200
Devon	Exeter	1,109,900
Dorset	Dorchester	701,900
Essex	Chelmsford	1,645,900
Gloucestershire	Gloucester	823,500
Greater London*		7,508,500
Greater Manchester*		2,547,700
Hampshire	Winchester	1,671,000
Herefordshire	Hereford	178,800
Hertfordshire	Hertford	1,048,200
Isle of Wight	Newport	140,000
Kent	Maidstone	1,621,000
Lancashire	Lancaster	1,439,200
Leicestershire	Leicester	915,800
Lincolnshire	Lincoln	993,300

* Metropolitan counties do not have an official county town.

Merseyside	Liverpool	1,367,200
Middlesex	Brentford, Clerkenwell or Westminster!	(included in Greater London)
Norfolk	Norwich	824,200
Northamptonshire	Northampton	651,800
Northumberland	Newcastle-upon-Tyne	311,400
Nottinghamshire	Nottingham	1,041,300
Oxfordshire	Oxford	626,900
Rutland	Oakham	37,300
Shropshire	Shrewsbury	450,700
Somerset	Taunton	884,400
Staffordshire	Stafford	1,055,000
Suffolk	Ipswich	692,100
Surrey	Guildford	1,075,600
Sussex (East)	Brighton	752,900
Sussex (West)	Chichester	764,300
Tyne and Wear*		1,095,200
Warwickshire	Warwick	533,900
West Midlands	Birmingham	2,591,300
Wiltshire	Trowbridge	630,700
Worcestershire	Worcester	555,900
Yorkshire	York	576,500 (East)
		1,045,000 (North)
		1,285,600 (South)
		2,118,600 (West)

(So who invented the South Riding, then? 'Riding' means 'one-third' and now we have four!)

R OBERT BYRON (the *other* Robert Byron, not the lord) was killed in the Second World War. He left behind a lot of writing, but to my mind nothing as moving as this. Count off the flowers, the moths and the butterflies and see how many you know. If I could hold on to just one piece of writing about the countryside, it would be this:

If I have a son, he shall salute the lords and ladies who un- furl green hoods to the March rains, and shall know them afterwards by their scarlet fruit. He shall know the celandine, and the frigid sightless flowers of the woods, spurge and spurge laurel, dog's mercury, wood sorrel and queer four-leaved herb-paris fit to trim a bonnet with its pur- ple dot. He shall see the marshes gold with flags and kingcups and find shepherd's purse on a slag heap. He shall know the tree flowers, scented lime tassels, blood-pink larch tufts, white strands of the Spanish chestnut and tattered oak plumes. He shall know orchids, mauve-winged bees and claret-coloured flies climbing up from mottled leaves. He shall see June red and white with ragged robin and cow pars- ley and the two campions. He shall tell a dandelion from sow thistle or goat's beard. He shall know the field flowers, lady's bedstraw and lady's slipper, purple mallow, blue chicory and the cranesbills – dusky, bloody and blue as heaven. In the cool summer wind he shall listen to the rattle of harebells against the whistle of a distant train, shall watch clover blush and scabious nod, pinch the ample vetches and savour the virgin turf. He shall know grasses, timothy and wag-wanton, and dust his fingertips in Yorkshire fog. By the river he shall know pink willow-herb and purple spikes of loosestrife, and the sweetshop smell of water mint where the rat dives silently from its hole. He shall know the velvet leaves and yellow spike of the old dowager, mullein, recognise the whole company of thistles, and greet the relatives of the nettle, wound-wort and hore-hound, yellow rattle, betony, bugle and archangel. In autumn, he shall know the hedge lanterns, hips and haws and bryony. At Christmas he shall climb an old apple tree for mistletoe, and know whom to kiss and how. He shall know the butterflies that suck the brambles, common whites and marbled white, orange-tip, brimstone, and the carnivorous clouded yellows. He shall watch fritillaries, pearl-bordered and silver-washed, flit like fireballs across the sunlit rides. He shall see that family of capitalists, peacock, painted lady, red admiral and the tortoiseshells, uncurl their trunks to suck blood from bruised plums, while the purple emperor and white admiral glut themselves on the bowels of a rabbit. He shall know the jagged comma, printed with a white c, the manx-tailed iridescent hair-streaks, and the skippers, demure as charwomen on a Monday morning. He shall run to the glint of silver on a chalk-hill blue – glint of a breeze on water beneath an open sky – and shall follow the brown explorers, meadow brown, brown argus, speckled wood and ringlet. He shall see death and revolution in the burnet moth, black and red, crawling from a house of yellow talc tied halfway up a tall grass. He shall know more rational moths, who like the night, the gaudy tigers, cream-spot and scarlet, and the red and yellow underwings. He shall hear the humming-bird hawk moth arrive like an air-raid on the garden at dusk, and know the other hawks, pink sleek-bodied elephant, poplar, lime and death's head. He shall count the pinions of the plume moths, and find the large emerald waiting in the rain-dewed grass.

All these I learnt when I was a child and each recalls a place or occasion that might otherwise be lost. They were my own discoveries. They taught me to look at the world with my own eyes and with attention. They gave me a first content with the universe. Town-dwellers lack this intimate content, but my son shall have it!

'All These I Learnt',
Robert Byron (1905–41)

British Butterflies

adonis blue
black hairstreak
brimstone
brown argus
brown hairstreak
chalkhill blue
chequered skipper
clouded yellow
comma
common blue
dark-green fritillary
dingy skipper
Duke of Burgundy fritillary
Essex skipper
gatekeeper
Glanville fritillary
grayling
green-veined white
green hairstreak
grizzled skipper

heath fritillary
high brown fritillary
holly blue
large blue

large copper
large heath
large skipper
large white
Lulworth skipper
marbled white
marsh fritillary
meadow brown
mountain ringlet
northern brown argus
swallowtail
orange tip
painted lady
peacock

pearl-bordered fritillary
purple emperor

Oh, to Be in England

purple hairstreak
red admiral
ringlet
Scotch argus
silver-spotted skipper
silver-studded blue
silver-washed fritillary
small blue
small copper
small heath
small pearl-bordered fritillary
small skipper
small tortoiseshell
small white
speckled wood
wall
white admiral
white-letter hairstreak
wood white

RANKING WITH ROBERT BYRON IN my affections is the Hampshire poet Edward Thomas, who was killed in the First World War. He wrote so many fine, if melancholic poems, but 'Adlestrop' is memorably evocative of a country station at the turn of the century. Alas, Dr Beeching did for most of the branch lines in the 1960s, but there is still one near me that has the quietness of Adlestrop.

Yes; I remember Adlestrop –
The name, because one afternoon
Of heat the express-train drew up there
Unwontedly. It was late June.

The steam hissed. Someone cleared his throat.
No one left and no one came
On the bare platform. What I saw
Was Adlestrop – only the name

And willows, willow-herb, and grass,
And meadowsweet, and haycocks dry,
No whit less still and lonely fair
Than the high cloudlets in the sky.

And for that minute a blackbird sang
Close by, and around him, mistier,
Farther and farther, all the birds
Of Oxfordshire and Gloucestershire.

'Adlestrop' (1917),
Edward Thomas (1878–1917)

'The Lincolnshire Poacher'

IN SPITE OF BEING AT SCHOOL in Yorkshire, we sang this traditional song in the local music festival. It would now be regarded as irresponsible to teach nine-year-olds about the delights of poaching, but Mrs Rishworth didn't seem to mind.

When I was bound apprentice in famous Lincolnshire,
Full well I served my master for more than seven years,
Till I took up to poaching, as you shall quickly hear,
Oh, 'tis my delight on a shiny night in the season of the year.

As me and my companions were setting of a snare,
'Twas then we spied the gamekeeper, for him we did not care,
Far we can wrestle and fight, my boys, and jump out anywhere,
Oh, 'tis my delight on a shiny night in the season of the year.

As me and my companions were setting four or five,
And taking on 'em up again, we caught a hare alive,
We took a hare alive, my boys, and through the woods did steer,
Oh, 'tis my delight on a shiny night in the season of the year.

Oh, to Be in England

I threw him on my shoulder and then we trudged home,
We took him to a neighbour's house, and sold him for a crown,
We sold him for a crown, my boys, but I did not tell you where,
Oh, 'tis my delight on a shiny night in the season of the year.

Success to ev'ry gentleman that lives in Lincolnshire,
Success to ev'ry poacher that wants to sell a hare,
Bad luck to ev'ry gamekeeper that will not sell his deer,
Oh, 'tis my delight on a shiny night in the season of the year.

'The Lincolnshire Poacher' (*c*.1776),
Anon.

A ND SO TO THE MORE WELL-KNOWN favourites. A. E.
Housman's *A Shropshire Lad* has many wonderful passages, but none more simple and beautiful than this:

> Loveliest of trees, the cherry now
> Is hung with bloom along the bough,
> And stands about the woodland ride
> Wearing white for Eastertide.
>
> Now, of my threescore years and ten,
> Twenty will not come again,
> And take from seventy springs a score,
> It only leaves me fifty more.
>
> And since to look at things in bloom
> Fifty springs are little room,
> About the woodlands I will go
> To see the cherry hung with snow.

'Loveliest of Trees, the Cherry Now' (1896),
A. E. Housman (1859–1936)

THE TROUBLE IS THAT TOO FEW of us take the time to look properly at the countryside. To stop and take it in. I guess you know what's coming …

> What is this life if, full of care,
> We have no time to stand and stare.
>
> No time to stand beneath the boughs
> And stare as long as sheep or cows.
>
> No time to see, when woods we pass,
> Where squirrels hide their nuts in grass.

> No time to see, in broad daylight,
> Streams of stars full, like skies at night.
>
> No time to turn at Beauty's glance,
> And watch her feet, how they can dance.
>
> No time to wait till her mouth can
> Enrich that smile her eyes began.

A poor life this if, full of care,
We have no time to stand and stare.

'Leisure' (1911),
William Henry Davies (1871–1940)

Those acquainted with the origin of surnames, and who have a knowledge of British poets, will observe that Mr Davies was a Welshman. With sentiments like these he must have wished he was English.

T HE MAN TO WHOM ALL NATURALISTS defer is the Reverend Gilbert White, who was curate at Selborne in
Hampshire. His *Natural History and Antiquities of Selborne*
has not been out of print since it was first published, in 1789.
It is still a really good read and reminds every modern naturalist of the need for curiosity and accurate observation.

As the swift eats, drinks, collects materials for its nest, and,
as it seems, propagates on the wing; it appears to live more
in the air than any other bird, and to perform all functions
there save those of sleeping and incubation.

This *hirundo* differs widely from its congeners in laying
invariably but two eggs at a time, which are milk-white,
long, and peaked at the small end; whereas the other species
lay at each brood from four to six. It is a most alert bird,
rising very early, and retiring to roost very late; and is on
the wing in the height of summer at least sixteen hours. In
the longest days it does not withdraw to rest till a quarter
before nine in the evening, being the latest of all day birds.
Just before they retire, whole groups of them assemble high
in the air, and squeak, and shoot about with wonderful
rapidity. But this bird is never so much alive as in sultry
thundery weather, when it expresses great alacrity, and calls
forth all its powers. In hot mornings several, getting together

in little parties, dash round the steeples and churches, squeaking as they go in a very clamorous manner: these, by nice observers, are supposed to be males serenading their sitting hens; and not without reason, since they seldom squeak till they come close to the walls or eaves, and since those within utter at the same time a little inward note of complacency.

The Natural History and Antiquities of Selborne (1789),
Rev. Gilbert White (1720–93)

ONE PERSON WHO COULD NEVER be accused of walking about oblivious to things was Sir John Betjeman. I share his love of Cornwall, and the images conjured up by his poem 'Trebetherick':

> We used to picnic where the thrift
>   Grew deep and tufted to the edge;
> We saw the yellow foam-flakes drift
>   In trembling sponges on the ledge
> Below us, till the wind would lift
>   Them up the cliff and o'er the hedge.
> Sand in the sandwiches, wasps in the tea,
> Sun on our bathing-dresses heavy with the wet,
> Squelch of the bladder-wrack waiting for the sea,
> Fleas round the tamarisk, an early cigarette.
>
> From where the coastguard houses stood
>   One used to see, below the hill,
> The lichened branches of a wood
>   In summer silver-cool and still;
> And there the Shade of Evil could
>   Stretch out at us from Shilla Mill.
> Thick with sloe and blackberry, uneven in the light,
> Lonely ran the hedge, the heavy meadow was remote,

England, Our England

The oldest part of Cornwall was the wood as black as night,
And the pheasant and the rabbit lay torn open at the throat.

But when a storm was at its height,
    And feathery slate was black in rain,
And tamarisks were hung with light,
    And golden sand was brown again,
Spring tide and blizzard would unite
    And sea came flooding up the lane.
Waves full of treasure then were roaring up the beach,
Ropes round our mackintoshes, waders warm and dry,
We waited for the wreckage to come swirling into reach,
Ralph, Vasey, Alastair, Biddy, John and I.

Then roller into roller curled
    And thundered down the rocky bay,
And we were in a water-world
    Of rain and blizzard, sea and spray,
And one against the other hurled
    We struggled round to Greenaway.
Blesséd be St Enodoc, blesséd be the wave,
Blesséd be the springy turf, we pray, pray to thee,
Ask for our children all the happy days you gave
To Ralph, Vasey, Alastair, Biddy, John and me.

'Trebetherick' (1940),
John Betjeman (1906–84)

The English Village

RONALD BLYTHE PAINTED A MOVING portrait of an English village in *Akenfield*. In it he allowed some of the locals to tell their own stories. They are often simple, but almost without exception they are affecting. The name of the village may be fictitious, but the people are real. The following extract is told by Sammy Whitelaw, aged fifty-eight, a farrier and bell-ringer:

I started ringing when I was fifteen – and walking too! Ringing and walking went together. The ringers from Cretingham would walk to Eye and those from Brandeston would walk to Woodbridge, and you'd get some ringers who would damn-near walk across England. That's a fact. You would meet them walking about all over Suffolk, looking for a good tower. Bell-mad, we were. I wasn't all that good. I could manage about 720 changes and that is about as far as I could go. Stedman started all this, you know. Most of the ringers I knew are dead and gone. I watched them, I did what they did, but it's a funny thing I couldn't ever do more than the 720 changes. I remember ringing one harvest time and the bell flew clean off the frame. Imagine that! Bell-tongues and our tongues stopped together then! 'That's a masterpiece!' old Charlie said. I can hear him saying it. The expert ringers used to call ringers like me 'turkey-drivers'. I didn't want to be a turkey-driver, but you can't always choose what you want to be in this mortal life. I knew a ringer who could ring the bell up once, make it wait, and catch a second toll as it came down. True. I wanted to do that but I couldn't.

I remember one cold November – I couldn't tell you how long ago – and a woman came to me and said, 'My Billy has passed, Sam. Ring the bell.' I said, 'How can I do that, ma'am? The tower has all been scaffolded for the repairs.' So off she went sorrowful. Then I had an idea. I climbed up into the bell-chamber, sat on the frame and banged the passing-bell with my hammer! I thought, old Billy won't mind. It was that bloody cold. But all could hear of the passing and take note.

Billy was one of the old people. The old people have gone and have taken a lot of truth out of the world with them. When Billy died, his wife walked down the garden and told the bees, and hung black crêpe on the hive. My grandfather did this, too. He said that if you didn't, the bees would die as well. Bees are dangerous to some folk and a gift to others. You'll get someone who'll get stung once and perish and another who'll get stung all over and get cured of all manner of things. There were a rare lot of bees in the village those days.

When they swarmed we used to all rush out into the garden with the fire-irons and scuttle and bang away; that brought them down.

I hope you like this village. I have lived here all my days and have been happy enough.

Akenfield: Portrait of an English Village (1969),
Ronald Blythe (1922–)

The Archers

THERE ARE THOSE WHOSE ONLY experience of country life is over the airwaves. They may take their lungful of fresh air from *Emmerdale* (they dropped the '*Farm*' bit several years ago now – it probably sounded too foreign) on ITV – or they can tune in every evening after the seven o'clock news on BBC Radio 4 for *The Archers*. When the series began, on the BBC Midlands Home Service on Whit Monday, 29 May 1950, it was subtitled 'an everyday story of country folk'. It was then networked across the country from 1 January 1951 at 11.45 a.m. on the Light Programme. By Easter the series was such a success that it was moved to 6.45 p.m. Its subtitle has long since gone. In fact, there is almost as much in the way of marital strife, discord and wife-swapping in Ambridge, the Borsetshire village, as there is in *Coronation Street* and *East-Enders*, and you'll rarely hear the current price of deadstock or the cost of a combine.

But *Archers* fans are die-hard types who will defend their heroes and heroines (and their villains and women-who-should-know-better) to the death. They do not want to know what the actors look like. They have vivid images in their heads of Shula and Brian, Usha and Eddie Grundy, and do not want their illusions shattered by reality.

And so I offer no pictures, just the list of current characters and the actors who play them. They deserve a bit of a perk for their stamina and durability, and also you might be surprised how many of them there are.

The Archers Cast*

Alice Aldridge – Hollie Chapman
Brian Aldridge – Charles Collingwood
Debbie Aldridge – Tamsin Greig
Jennifer Aldridge – Angela Piper
Marjorie Antrobus – Margot Boyd
David Archer – Timothy Bentinck
Helen Archer – Louiza Patikas
Jill Archer – Patricia Greene
Kenton Archer – Richard Attlee
Pat Archer – Patricia Gallimore
Phil Archer – Norman Painting
Pip Archer – Helen Monks
Ruth Archer – Felicity Finch
Tom Archer – Tom Graham
Tony Archer – Colin Skipp
Christine Barford – Lesley Saweard

*As at summer 2007.

Lilian Bellamy – Sunny Ormonde
Lewis Carmichael – Robert Lister
Christopher Carter – William Sanderson-Thwaite
Neil Carter – Brian Hewlett
Susan Carter – Charlotte Martin
Ian Craig – Stephen Kennedy
Matt Crawford – Kim Durham
Wayne Foley – Ian Brooker
Alan Franks – John Telfer
Amy Franks – Vinette Robinson
Bert Fry – Eric Allan
Clarrie Grundy – Rosalind Adams
Ed Grundy – Barry Farrimond
Eddie Grundy – Trevor Harrison
Emma Grundy – Felicity Jones
Joe Grundy – Edward Kelsey
Will Grundy – Philip Molloy
Shiv Gupta – Shiv Grewel
Usha Gupta – Souad Faress
Daniel Hebden Lloyd – Dominic Davies
Shula Hebden Lloyd – Judy Bennett
Izzy – Elizabeth Wofford
Jason the builder – Brian Miller
Jazzer – Ryan Kelly
Satya Khanna – Jamila Massey
Alistair Lloyd – Michael Lumsden

Oh, to Be in England

Adam Macy – Andrew Wincott
Kate Madikane – Kellie Bright
Kirsty Miller – Annabelle Dowler
Elizabeth Pargetter – Alison Dowling
Nigel Pargetter – Graham Seed
Jolene Perks – Buffy Davis
Kathy Perks – Hedli Niklaus
Sid Perks – Alan Devereux
Heather Pritchard – Joyce Gibbs
Fallon Rogers – Joanna van Kampen
Graham Ryder – Malcolm McKee
Lynda Snell – Carole Boyd
Robert Snell – Graham Blockey
Caroline Sterling – Sara Coward
Oliver Sterling – Michael Cochrane
Mabel Thompson – Mona Hammond
Brenda Tucker – Amy Shindler
Hayley Tucker – Lorraine Coady
Mike Tucker – Terry Molloy
Roy Tucker – Ian Pepperell
Jack Woolley – Arnold Peters
Peggy Woolley – June Spencer

'Widdecombe Fair'

WIDDECOMBE-IN-THE-MOOR is a delightful Devon village in the middle of Dartmoor, with a handsome church (and a teashop or two) at its heart. Visit it, and the famous Tors (rock outcrops), and sing the song as you do so.

1. Tom Pearce, Tom Pearce, lend me your grey mare,
    All along down along out along lee,
    For I want for to go to Widdecombe Fair.

Chorus
Wi' Bill Brewer, Jan Stewer,
Peter Gurney, Peter Davey,
Dan'l Whiddon, Harry Hawke,
Old Uncle Tom Cobbley and all,
Old Uncle Tom Cobbley and all.

2. And when shall I see again my grey mare,
    All along down along out along lee,
    By Friday soon or Saturday noon.
    Chorus

3. Then Friday came and Saturday noon,
   All along down along out along lee,
   But Tom Pearce's old mare hath not trotted home.
   Chorus

4. So Tom Pearce, he got up to the top of the hill,
   All along down along out along lee,
   And he seed his old mare down a making her will.
   Chorus

5. So Tom Pearce's old mare, her took sick and died,
   All along down along out along lee,
   And Tom, he sat down on a stone and he cried.
   Chorus

6. And all the night long be heard skirling and groans,
   All along down along out along lee,
   From Tom Pearce's old mare and the rattling bones of.
   Chorus

7. When the wind whistles cold on the moor of a night,
   All along down along out along lee,
   Tom Pearce's old mare doth appear ghastly white.
   Chorus

'Widdecombe Fair' (date unknown),
Anon.

England Wouldn't Be England Without

the Queen
allotments
picnics
bell-ringers
cucumber sandwiches (no crusts)
daisies in the lawn

Miss Marple
Morris dancers
queuing
Jane Austen
the National Trust
Thomas Rowlandson
cream teas
grass tennis courts
scouting
wet bank holidays

Oh, to Be in England

Hogarth
the boat race
the Isle of Wight
hunting
Ascot

roast beef and Yorkshire pudding
well dressing
Haratio, Lord Nelson
Sloane Rangers
bluebell woods
P. G. Wodehouse
agricultural shows
Isambard Kingdom Brunel
inglenooks
knotted handkerchiefs
greenhouses
morning dress
Elgar
village greens
the Routemaster bus
Fortnum and Mason
the Lake District
J. M. W. Turner

England, Our England

pipes and slippers
meadows with buttercups
Charles Dickens
Marks and Spencer
antimacassars
Cornish pasties
the Proms
Number 10
Ivor Novello
bowler hats
Fisherman's Friend lozenges
Glyndebourne
the *Daily Telegraph*
Cowes Week
Edward Seago
the Derby
beehives
the Season
Melton Mowbray Pork Pies
Winston Churchill
twenty-one-gun salutes
the Royal Academy Summer Exhibition
seagulls
Crown Green Bowling
the Burlington Arcade
Chatsworth

Oh, to Be in England

'The Lark Ascending'
fish and chips and mushy peas
Hampton Court
Thomas Gainsborough
glorious Goodwood
the Shipping Forecast
Osborne House
Blackpool rock
Beefeaters
the Cotswolds
the Grand National
bantams
steam railways
the Garter Service
Agatha Christie
donkey rides
Trooping the Colour
policemen in shirtsleeves
the Lord's Test Match
George Stubbs
Morris Minors
Chewton Glen
Radox
Twickenham
Badminton Horse Trials
Smythson of Bond Street

Samuel Pepys
polo
Rev. Gilbert White
real ale
the National Gardens Scheme
Oxbridge
John Clare
Hatchards
the Beatles
meat pies
cheese and pickle sandwiches
cricket matches
the Sunday papers
duck ponds
The Mousetrap
Alan Bennett
red pillar boxes
sheds
churchyards
egg sandwiches
Oliver Cromwell
cornfields with poppies
Eton mess
Eton
the Prince of Wales
amateur dramatics

Oh, to Be in England

Cadbury's Dairy Milk
black cabs
beefeaters
Gardeners' Question Time
cheese-rolling
A. J. Munnings
Wimbledon
Chelsea Flower Show
pubs
bacon sandwiches
public libraries
Sunday walks
flat caps
the WI
ploughman's lunches
punting
Savile Row
Radio 3
Bath
a bath
John Constable
Stonehenge
weird village names like Barnoldswick and Piddletrenthide
The Beano
the Dowager Duchess of Devonshire
the Globe Theatre

England, Our England

Henley Royal Regatta
Coronation Street
Betty's Cafe
Guy Fawkes Night
maypoles
animal rescue centres
church choirs
gymkhanas
Ilkley Moor
village fêtes
leaves on the line
Oliver Cromwell
Gilbert and Sullivan
and
the weather.

*It is pure unadulterated country life. They get up
early because they have so much to do and go to bed
early because they have so little to think about.*

The Picture of Dorian Gray (1891),
Oscar Wilde (1854–1900)

ALFRED WAINWRIGHT MADE A PLAN not only to climb all the fells of Lakeland, but to draw them and write his own guidebooks. Each one is a work of art, as well as a practical handbook, and there are others such as the *Pennine Way Companion* and *Walks in Limestone Country* that are every bit as good. Treat yourself to the set – if you can find them.

Here he is in *Fell Wanderer*, with eminently practical tips on walking, delivered in that no-nonsense A.J.W. way:

Clumsy walking is the cause of accidents. If clumsy walkers did no more than damage themselves they would be welcome to go on doing it, but they also spoil the paths for everybody else. Bulls in china shops are gentle creatures compared with some of the pedestrians one sees, and hears, in Rossett Gill or Little Hell Gate or Lord's Rake. They are often verbally noisy, a common characteristic of the inefficient, but it is their boots that cause most clatter. Flying stones, uprooted sods and blasphemous shouts accompany their sliding progress, especially downhill, in a surround of noise. At home, one imagines, there will not be a cup with a handle, not a chair without broken springs, not a door with a knob left on. But a good walker moves silently and is a joy to behold. He moves not gracefully, but rhythmically. His footstep is firm. He presses the path into place with his boots, and improves it. The clumsy walker loosens and destroys paths. A good walker loves the zigzags of a path, which always give the easiest progression, but a bad walker can't be bothered, cuts across them and ruins them for others. A good walker always gives the impression of moving leisurely, even slowly, and having time to spare; a bad walker always seems to be in a hurry. A good walker will climb Scafell Pike from Sty Head and hardly disturb a single stone; a bad walker will leave a trail of debris. Their respective journeys through life will be the same.

I have mentioned boots, and might borrow Kipling's song title to emphasise the word thrice, because boots are the best footgear for the hills. But wear shoes or sandals or go barefoot if any of these suit you better. Reams have been written on what to wear on the hills, but ignore such advice. The thing is to wear what is most comfortable. It is a matter of individual choice; don't be dictated to. Clothes never become comfortable until they are shabby and shapeless and well perforated by sparks from the pipe; at least, mine don't, and when you can no longer appear at the office in them without shame they are ready to serve you on the hills, where nobody is there to see them and wouldn't bother if they did. Comfort is the thing. Comfort includes keeping warm and dry, but ways of achieving it differ widely. The most ghastly apparitions appear on the fells, spectral creatures and scarecrows on two legs, representing varying conceptions of the ideal mountain garb. If sheep didn't have such good manners they would laugh their heads off. Clothing is an individual matter. You don't have to look like the man in front. As with everything else, one learns from experience.

A lot of advice has been given by various authorities on equipment: the need for taking a map and compass and a whistle (they never mention guidebooks, drat them!), on stoves and cooking gear, on exposure meters and lenses and filters and so on. And a lot of rot has been said. Well, please yourself if you want to carry a load of hardware and ironmongery around, but don't make fellwalking a game to be played by rules. It is a pleasure, as I have said, or it is not fellwalking at all; it is something to enjoy or something to endure: it cannot be both. You see hikers setting forth for a day on the hills burdened as though they were starting a six-month expedition to Antarctica: they are grim and anguished of face when they ought to be carefree and smiling. They are not going into uncharted wastes and should have no more sense of apprehension or impending risk than if they were going for a Sunday-afternoon stroll in the park. The hills are friendly: there are no lurking hazards, no traps around every corner. The dangers have been absurdly exaggerated; there are too many gloomy prophets around, and too many people ready with advice, including me. You are not making a date with death. You are not making a technical excursion into space. You are going for a walk, that's all, no different from all other walks except that there is more up and down and the way is likely to be rougher, and you are going to see and enjoy beautiful scenery, wild and lonely places and visions of loveliness that will bring tears to your eyes and joy to your heart at the same time; but you are far more likely to run into danger crossing the main street of Keswick. If you get into trouble on the fells it will be your own fault; in the main street of Keswick it might not be. The fells are not monsters, but amiable giants. You can romp over them and pull the hairs on their chests and shout in their ears and treat them rough, and they don't mind a bit. They are not enemies to be wrestled with. They are friends. Go amongst them as you go amongst friends.

Fell Wanderer (1966),
Alfred Wainwright (1907–91)

'On Ilkla Moor Baht 'At'

A S A NATIVE OF ILKLEY, I HAVE to include my native anthem. 'Baht 'at' simply means 'without a hat'. Ilkley Moor is a draughty place. You'll get the drift, and your accent will improve.

Wheear 'as ta bin sin ah saw thee,
On Ilkla Moor baht 'at?
Wheear 'as ta bin sin ah saw thee?
Wheear 'as ta bin sin ah saw thee?
On Ilkla Moor baht 'at?
On Ilkla Moor baht 'at?
On Ilkla Moor baht 'at?

Tha's been a cooartin' Mary Jane
On Ilkla Moor baht 'at;
Tha's been a cooartin' Mary Jane,
Tha's been a cooartin' Mary Jane,
On Ilkla Moor baht 'at,
On Ilkla Moor baht 'at,
On Ilkla Moor baht 'at.

The verses continue in this fashion with the following lines:

> Tha's bahn t'catch thi deeath o'cowd
>
> Then we shall ha' to bury thee
>
> Then t'worms 'll cum an' eat thee oop
>
> Then t'ducks 'll cum an' eat oop t'worms
>
> Then we shall go an' eat oop t'ducks
>
> Then we shall all 'ave etten thee.

THE LAST WORD HERE GOES to Richard Jefferies, a writer whose book *The Life of the Fields* was published at the end of the nineteenth century. His books *The Gamekeeper at Home* and *The Amateur Poacher* will give you a flavour of the man – a practical countryman to the core, whose style of writing is one we have lost. No commentators today dare be as enthusiastic or as emotional in their writings. Or maybe in the twenty-first century we are just more restrained; more cautious of eulogising lest it be taken for gush. Sad, really. Jefferies is not afraid to luxuriate in the countryside and to express his delight at its rich diversity. Is that such a bad thing?

I cannot leave it; I must stay under the old tree in the midst of the long grass, the luxury of the leaves, and the song in the very air. I seem as if I could feel all the glowing life the sunshine gives and the south wind calls to being. The endless grass, the endless leaves, the immense strength of the oak expanding, the unalloyed joy of finch and blackbird; from all of them I receive a little. Each gives me something of the pure joy they gather for themselves. In the blackbird's melody one note is mine; in the dance of the leaf shadows the formed maze is for me, though the motion is theirs; the flowers with a thousand faces have collected the kisses of the morning. Feeling with them, I receive some, at least, of their fullness of life. Never could I have enough; never stay long enough – whether here or whether lying on the shorter sward under the sweeping and graceful birches, or on the thyme-scented hills. Hour after hour, and still not enough. On walking, the footpath was never long enough or my strength sufficient to endure till the mind was weary. The

exceeding beauty of the earth, in her splendour of life, yields a new thought with every petal. The hours when the mind is absorbed by beauty are the only hours when we really live, so that the longer we can stay among these things, so much the more is snatched from inevitable Time. Let the shadow advance upon the dial – I can watch it with equanimity while it is there to be watched. It is only when the shadow is *not* there, when the clouds of winter cover it, that the dial is terrible. The invisible shadow goes on and steals from us. But now, while I can see the shadow of the tree and watch it slowly gliding along the surface of the grass, it is mine. These are the only hours that are not wasted – these hours that absorb the soul and fill it with beauty. This is real life, and all else is illusion, or mere endurance. Does this reverie of flowers and waterfall and song form an ideal, a human ideal, in the mind? It does; much the same ideal that Phidias sculptured of man and woman filled with a godlike sense of the violet fields of Greece, beautiful beyond thought, calm as my turtledove before the lurid lightning of the unknown. To be beautiful and to be calm, without mental fear, is the ideal of nature. If I cannot achieve it, at least I can think it.

The Life of the Fields (1884),
Richard Jefferies (1848–87)

Oranges and Lemons

THE TOWNIE, OF COURSE, FEELS NERVOUS in the country. It's full of noise (cows and pigs and sheep and tractors) and smells (dog roses, wild garlic and manure). He feels safer in the city, where there are civilised things like traffic lights and left filters, pavement cafés and Chelsea tractors, and where passers-by don't meet your eye.

I met a woman a while ago – she was accompanying me on a book tour – and she asked me what it was like living in a village. She lived in North London.

'What do you mean?' I asked.

'Well,' she said, 'what do you do when people say "Hello"?'

'I say "Hello" back.'

'But how do you get away?'

The prospect of being trapped by a stranger filled her with genuine horror.

The Bells of London Town

I STILL HAVE THE LITTLE CUT-OUT BOOK I was given when I was little, 'arranged and illustrated by Molly B. Thompson'. This is the rhyme that taught me all I knew about London at the age of four or five:

Gay go up and gay go down,
To ring the bells of London Town.
'Brickbats and tiles,'
Say the bells of St Giles'.
'Bull's-eyes and targets,'
Say the bells of St Margaret's.
'Pokers and tongs,'
Say the bells of St John's.
'Oranges and lemons,'
Say the bells of St Clement's.
'Kettles and pans,'
Say the bells of St Anne's.
'Old Father Baldpate,'
Say the slow bells of Aldgate.

Oranges and Lemons

'Two sticks and an apple,'
Say the bells of Whitechapel.
'Halfpence and farthings,'
Say the bells of St Martin's.
'Pancakes and fritters,'
Say the bells of St Peter's.
'You owe me ten shillings,'
Say the bells of St Helen's.
'When will you pay me?'
Say the bells of Old Bailey.
'When I grow rich,'
Say the bells of Shoreditch.
'When will that be?'
Say the bells of Stepney.
'I'm sure I don't know,'
Says the great bell of Bow.
Gay go up and gay go down
To ring the bells of London Town.

'Oranges and Lemons' (c.1665),
Anon.

London Pride has been handed down to us.
London Pride is a flower that's free.
London Pride means our own dear town to us,
And our pride it for ever will be.

Grey city,
Stubbornly implanted,
Taken so for granted
For a thousand years.
Stay, city,
Smokily enchanted,
Cradle of our memories and hopes and fears.

Every Blitz
Your resistance
Toughening,
From the Ritz
To the Anchor and Crown,
Nothing ever could override
The pride of London Town.

'London Pride' (1941),
Noël Coward (1899–1973)

Earth has not anything to show more fair:
Dull would he be of soul who could pass by
A sight so touching in its majesty:
This City now doth, like a garment, wear
The beauty of the morning: silent, bare,
Ships, towers, domes, theatres, and temples lie
Open unto the fields, and to the sky,
All bright and glittering in the smokeless air.
Never did sun more beautifully steep
In his first splendour, valley, rock, or hill;
Ne'er saw I, never felt, a calm so deep!
The river glideth at his own sweet will:
Dear God! the very houses seem asleep;
And all that mighty heart is lying still!

'Upon Westminster Bridge' (1802),
William Wordsworth (1770–1850)

Londoners have a reputation for being stoic in the face of all difficulties. They have had plenty of practice. Samuel Pepys (1633–1703) records the famous incident of the Great Fire of London in his diary, bringing the images of that historic conflagration vividly to life:

September

2. *Lords day*. Some of our maids sitting up late last night to get things ready against our feast today, Jane called us up, about 3 in the morning, to tell us of a great fire they saw in the City. So I rose, and slipped on my nightgown and went to her window, and thought it to be on the back side of Markelane at the furthest; but being unused to such fires as fallowed, I thought it far enough off, and so went to bed again and to sleep. About 7 rose again to dress myself, and there looked out at the window and saw the fire not so much as it was, and further off. So to my closet to set things to rights after yesterday's cleaning. By and by Jane comes and tells me that she hears that above 300 houses have been burned down tonight by the fire we saw, and that it was now burning down all Fishstreet by London Bridge. So I made myself ready presently, and walked to the Tower and there got up upon one of the high places, Sir J. Robinsons little

son going up with me; and there I did see the houses at that
end of the bridge all on fire, and an infinite great fire on this
and the other side the end of the bridge – which, among
other people, did trouble me for poor little Michell and our
Sarah on the Bridge. So down, with my heart full of trouble,
to the Lieutenant of the Tower, who tells me that it begun
this morning in the King's bakers house in Pudding lane, and
that it hath burned down St. Magnes Church and most part
of Fishstreete already. So I down to the waterside and there
got a boat and through the bridge, and there saw a lament-
able fire. Poor Michells house, as far as the Old Swan, already
burned that way and the fire running further, that in a very
little time it got as far as the Stillyard while I was there.
Everybody endeavouring to remove their goods, and flinging
into the River or bringing them into lighters that lay off.
Poor people staying in their houses as long as till the very
fire touched them, and then running into boats or clamber-
ing from one pair of stair by the waterside to another. And
among other things, the poor pigeons I perceive were loath
to leave their houses, but hovered about the windows and
balconies till they were some of them burned, their wings,
and fell down.

Having stayed, and in an hour's time seen the fire rage
every way, and nobody to my sight endeavouring to quench
it, but to remove their goods and leave all to the fire; and
having seen it get as far as the Steeleyard, and the wind

mighty high and driving it into the city, and everything, after so long a drougth, proving combustible, even the very stones of churches, and among other things, the poor steeple by which pretty Mrs. [Horsley] lives, and whereof my old schoolfellow Elborough is parson, taken fire in the very top and there burned till it fall down – I to Whitehall with a gentleman with me who desired to go off from the Tower to see the fire in my boat – to Whitehall, and there up to the King's closet in the chapel, where people came about me and I did give them an account dismayed them all; and word was carried in to the King, so I was called for and did tell the King and Duke of York what I saw, and that unless his Majesty did command houses to be pulled down, nothing could stop the fire. They seemed much troubled, and the King commanded me to go to my Lord Mayor from him and command him to spare no houses but to pull down before the fire every way. The Duke of York bid me tell him that if he would have any more soldiers, he shall; and so did my Lord Arlington afterward, as a great secret. Here meeting with Capt. Cocke, I in his coach, which he lent me, and Creed with me, to Pauls; and there walked along Watling street as well as I could, every creature coming away loaden with goods to save – and here and there sick people carried away in beds. Extraordinary good goods carried in carts and on backs. At last met my Lord Mayor in Canning Streete, like a man spent, with a handkercher about his neck. To the King's message, he cried like a fainting woman, 'Lord, what can I do? I am spent! People will not obey me. I have been pull[ing] down houses. But the fire overtakes us faster then we can do it.' That he needed no more soldiers; and that for himself, he must go and refresh himself, having been up all night. So he left me, and I him, and walked home – seeing people all almost distracted and no manner of means used to quench the fire. The houses too, so very thick thereabouts, and full of matter for burning, as pitch and tar, in Thames street – and warehouses of oyle and wines and Brandy and other things. Here I saw Mr. Isaccke Houblon, that handsome man – prettily dressed and dirty at his door at Dowgate, receiving some of his brothers things whose houses were on fire; and as he says, have been removed twice already, and he doubts (as it soon proved) that they must be in a little time removed from his house also – which was a sad consideration. And to see the churches all filling with goods, by people who themselfs should have been quietly there at this time. By this time it was about 12 a-clock, and so home and there find my guests, which was Mr. Wood and his wife, Barbary Shelden, and also Mr. Moone – she mighty fine, and her husband, for aught I see, a likely man. But Mr. Moones design and mine, which was to look over my closet and please him with the sight thereof, which he hath long desired, was wholly disappointed, for we were in great trouble and disturbance at this fire, not knowing what to think of it. However, we had an extraordinary good dinner, and as merry as at this time we could be. While at dinner, Mrs. Batelier came to enquire after Mr. Woolfe and Stanes (who it seems are related to them), whose houses in Fishstreet are all burned, and they in a sad condition. She would not stay in the fright.

As soon as dined, I and Moone away and walked through the City, the streets full of nothing but people and horses and carts loaden with goods, ready to run over one another, and removing goods from one burned house to another – they now removing out of Canning street (which received goods in the morning) into Lumbard Streete and further; and among others, I now saw my little goldsmith Stokes receiving some friend's goods, whose house itself was burned the day after. We parted at Pauls, he home and I to Pauls Wharf, where I had appointed a boat to attend me; and took in Mr. Carcasse and his brother, whom I met in the street, and carried them below and above bridge, to and again, to see the fire, which was now got further, both below and above, and no likelihood of stopping it. Met with the King and Duke of York in their Barge, and with them to Queen Hith and there called Sir Rd. Browne to them. Their order was only to pull down houses apace, and so below bridge at the waterside; but little was or could be done, the fire coming upon them so fast. Good hopes there was of stopping it at the Three Cranes above, and at Buttolphs Wharf below bridge, if care be used; but the wind carries it into the City, so as we know not by the waterside what it doth there. River full of lighter[s] and boats taking in goods, and good goods swimming in the water; and only, I observed that hardly one lighter or boat in three that had goods of a house in, but there was a pair of virginalls in it. Having seen as much as I could now, I away to Whitehall by appointment, and there walked to St. James's Park, and there met my wife and Creed and Wood and his wife and walked to my boat, and there upon the water again, and to the fire up and down, it still increasing and the wind great. So near the fire as we could for smoke; and all over the Thames, with one's face in the wind you were almost burned with a shower of Firedrops – this is very true – so as houses were burned by these drops and flakes of fire, three or four, nay five or six houses, one from another. When we could endure no more upon the water, we to a little alehouse on the Bankside over against the Three Cranes, and there stayed till it was dark almost and saw the fire grow; and as it grow darker, appeared more and more, and in Corners and upon steeples and between churches and houses, as far as we could see up the hill of the City, in a most horrid malicious bloody flame, not like the fine flame of an ordinary fire. Barbary and her husband away before us. We stayed till, it being darkish, we saw the fire as only one entire arch of fire from this to the other side of the bridge, and in a bow up the hill, for an arch of above a mile long. It made me weep to see it. The churches, houses, and

all on fire and flaming at once, and a horrid noise the flames
made, and the cracking of houses at their ruine.

from *The Diary of Samuel Pepys*
2nd September 1666
(Penguin Books, 1987)

WE COMPLAIN ABOUT LONDON TODAY, but should be heartened to know that it has been much worse. If going to the theatre is a bit of a headache thanks to transport arrangements, there was a time, four hundred or so years ago, when it was positively life-threatening ...

Of the many straightforward manuals teaching social survival perhaps Henry Peacham's is the most beguiling. His approach is not ironic. The book is a serious attempt to prevent innocent visitors to big cities from being instantly parted from their money. But his touch is light:

Take a private chamber wherein you may pass your spare time in doing something or other, and what you call for, pay for, without going upon the score, especially in city ale-houses, where in many places you shall be torn out of your skin, if it were possible, even for a debt of twopence ...

Keep out of throngs and public places where multitudes of people are – for saving your purse. The fingers of a number go beyond your sense of feeling. A tradesman's wife of the Exchange one day, when her husband was following some business in the city, desired him he would give her leave to go see a play, which she had not done in seven years. He bade her take his apprentice along with her and go, but especially to have a care of her purse, which she warranted him she would. Sitting in a box among some gallants and gallant wenches and returning when the play was done, she returned to her husband and told him she had lost her purse.

'Wife,' quoth he, 'did I not give you warning of it? How much money was there in it?'

Quoth she, 'Truly, four pieces, six shillings, and a silver toothpicker.'

Quoth her husband, 'Where did you put it?'

'Under my petticoat, between that and my smock.'

'What,' quoth he, 'did you feel nobody's hand there?'

'Yes,' quoth she, 'I felt one's hand there, but I did not think he had come for that.'

So much for the guard of the purse.

Henry Peacham (1576–1643?), *The Art of Living in London* (1642)
from *The Oxford Book of Humorous Prose*
(Oxford University Press, 1990)

Season of Mists and Mellow Fruitfulness

ONE OF THE PLEASURES OF LIVING IN England is the variation in the seasons. The tropics are all very well, but all that bougainvillea, oleander and plumbago does begin to pall when it's sitting there looking at you every blessed day of the year. No; give me a hard winter, a showery spring, a warm summer and a damp autumn and I'm happy. All right, so it is sometimes a damp winter, a damp spring, a damp summer and a damp autumn, but at least it's unpredictable. Usually.

> January brings the snow,
> Makes your feet and fingers glow.
>
> February's ice and sleet,
> Freeze the toes right off your feet.
>
> Welcome March, with wint'ry wind,
> Would thou wer not so unkind.
>
> April brings the sweet spring showers,
> On and on for hours and hours.

Farmers fear unkindly May,
Frost by night and hail by day.

June just rains and never stops,
Thirty days and spoils the crops.

In July the sun is hot.
Is it shining? No, it's not!

August, cold and dank and wet
Brings more rain than any yet.

Bleak September's mist and mud
Is enough to chill the blood.

Then October adds a gale,
Wind and slush and rain and hail.

Dark November brings the fog,
Should not do it to a dog.

Freezing wet December, then ...
Bloody January again!

'A Song for the Weather' (1956),
Michael Flanders (1922–75) and Donald Swann (1923–94)

DAFFODILS, THOUGH, YOU CAN ALWAYS rely on, even though nowadays they are blooming several weeks earlier than they did in Wordsworth's time. (You will be pleased to know that there is not a single mention of global warming anywhere else in this book.)

> I wandered lonely as a cloud
> That floats on high o'er vales and hills,
> When all at once I saw a crowd,
> A host, of golden daffodils;
> Beside the lake, beneath the trees
> Fluttering and dancing in the breeze.
>
> Continuous as the stars that shine
> And twinkle on the milky way,
> They stretched in never-ending line
> Along the margin of a bay:
> Ten thousand saw I at a glance,
> Tossing their heads in sprightly dance.
>
> The waves beside them danced, but they
> Out-did the sparkling waves in glee:
> A Poet could not but be gay
> In such a jocund company!

I gazed – and gazed – but little thought
What wealth the show to me had brought.

For oft, when on my couch I lie
In vacant or in pensive mood,
They flash upon that inward eye
Which is the bliss of solitude;
And then my heart with pleasure fills,
And dances with the daffodils.

'Daffodils' (ed. 1813),
William Wordsworth (1770–1850)

ND HERE'S THE DAMP ONE, courtesy of John Keats:

Season of mists and mellow fruitfulness,
  Close bosom-friend of the maturing sun;
Conspiring with him how to load and bless
  With fruit the vines that round the thatch-eaves run;
To bend with apples the mossed cottage-trees,
  And fill all fruit with ripeness to the core;
    To swell the gourd, and plump the hazel shells
  With a sweet kernel; to set budding more,
And still more, later flowers for the bees,
Until they think warm days will never cease,
    For Summer has o'er-brimmed their clammy cells.

Who hath not seen thee oft amid thy store?
  Sometimes whoever seeks abroad may find
Thee sitting careless on a granary floor,
  Thy hair soft-lifted by the winnowing wind;
Or on a half-reaped furrow sound asleep,
  Drowsed with the fume of poppies while thy hook
    Spares the next swath and all its twinèd flowers;
And sometimes like a gleaner thou dost keep
  Steady thy laden head across a brook;

Or by a cider-press, with patient look,
    Thou watchest the last oozings hours by hours.

Where are the songs of Spring? Ay, where are they?
    Think not of them, thou hast thy music too,
While barred clouds bloom the soft-dying day,
    And touch the stubble-plains with rosy hue;
Then in a wailful choir the small gnats mourn
    Among the river sallows, borne aloft
      Or sinking as the light wind lives or dies;
And full-grown lambs loud bleat from hilly bourn;
    Hedge-crickets sing; and now with treble soft
    The red-breast whistles from a garden-croft;
      And gathering swallows twitter in the skies.

'To Autumn' (1820),
John Keats (1795–1821)

The Weather

ACCORDING TO THE REST of the world, we are obsessed with it. But then, we have a lot of it to be obsessed with. That's why we have weather forecasts on the hour, every hour. But do we understand them?

Here are a few terms that might help:

sunny spells – mainly cloudy

scattered showers – continuous rain

a warm front – bikini weather

a cold front – one that is well wrapped up

an occluded front – one button undone

unsettled – continuous rain

an anticyclone – your mother's sister's bike that only comes out in fair weather

precipitation – anything that falls out of the sky, apart from aircraft

spits and spots – just because your granny's got it, it doesn't mean to say you're going to get it. (*See also* 'scattered showers'.)

fifty per cent chance of a shower – if it rains, I was right; if it doesn't rain, I was right

rain – falling water
snow – frozen falling water
hail – frozen falling water that hurts
high pressure – likely to make you perspire
low pressure – keep your coat on
imminent – already happening
soon – already happening
later – soon
gale warnings – excuses for the high price of fish

Water, Water Everywhere

WE ARE AN ISLAND RACE with an inherent love of the sea. Well, most of us love it. There are those who get seasick at the sight of a duck pond, but for most of us, the tang of salt air, the sea breeze in our hair and the sound of the crashing waves is mother's milk.

I must down to the seas again, to the lonely sea and the sky,
And all I ask is a tall ship and a star to steer her by,
And the wheel's kick and the wind's song and the white sail's
    shaking,
And a grey mist on the sea's face and a grey dawn breaking.

I must down to the seas again, for the call of the running tide
Is a wild call and a clear call that may not be denied;
And all I ask is a windy day with the white clouds flying,
And the flung spray and the blown spume, and the sea-gulls crying.

I must down to the seas again, to the vagrant gypsy life,
To the gull's way and the whale's way where the wind's like a
    whetted knife;
And all I ask is a merry yarn from a laughing fellow-rover,
And quiet sleep and a sweet dream when the long trick's over.

'Sea-Fever' (1902), Sir John Masefield (1878–1967)

AND WE DREAM OF SAILING AWAY on a boat. A boat with a romantic name …

> Quinquireme of Nineveh from distant Ophir,
> Rowing home to haven in sunny Palestine,
> With a cargo of ivory,
> And apes and peacocks,
> Sandalwood, cedarwood, and sweet white wine.
>
> Stately Spanish galleon coming from the Isthmus,
> Dipping through the Tropics by the palm-green shores,
> With a cargo of diamonds,
> Emeralds, amethysts,
> Topazes, and cinnamon and gold moidores.
>
> Dirty British coaster with a salt-caked smoke-stack
> Butting through the Channel in the mad March days,
> With a cargo of Tyne coal,
> Road-rail, pig-lead,
> Firewood, iron-ware, and cheap tin trays.

'Cargoes' (1903),
Sir John Masefield (1878–1967)

Sea Areas

⁂

SEA AREAS ARE THOSE mysterious-sounding parts of the North Sea and the Atlantic that are quoted in that famous litany that is the Shipping Forecast. There were changes a few years ago when one or two of the boundaries were redrawn and Finisterre became Fitzroy.

The Shipping Forecast is broadcast each day on BBC Radio 4 at 00.48, 05.20, 12.00 and 17.54 hours. Each bulletin contains 350 words and begins with warnings of gales (when they are issued) followed by a general summary of current weather conditions known as the 'general synopsis'. This is in turn followed by the forecasts for the sea areas around the UK – 'the area forecasts for the next twenty-four hours'. Areas are named in a clockwise direction and followed by 'weather reports from coastal stations', also given in a clockwise direction.

The reports give the current barometric pressure and trend (rising, falling or steady), wind direction and force, current weather (rain, showers, etc.) and visibility (fog, poor, moderate or good). My little hand-drawn sea area map is on the next page.

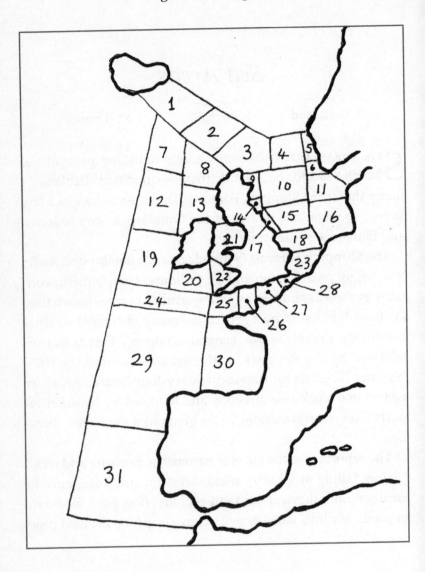

Sea Areas

1. S. E. Iceland	12. Rockall	23. Thames
2. Faeroes	13. Malin	24. Sole
3. Fair Isle	14. Forth	25. Plymouth
4. Viking	15. Dogger	26. Portland
5. N. Utsire	16. German Bight	27. Wight
6. S. Utsire	17. Tyne	28. Dover
7. Bailey	18. Humber	29. Fitzray
8. Hebrides	19. Shannon	30. Biscay
9. Cromarty	20. Fastnet	31. Trafalgar
10. Forties	21. Irish Sea	
11. Fisher	22. Lundy	

Gale warnings

WARNING	BEAUFORT SCALE	SPEED (KNOTS)
Gale	8	34–40
Severe gale	9	41–47
Storm	10	48–55
Violent storm	11	56–63
Hurricane	12	More than 64

Time periods

DESCRIPTION	MEANING
Imminent	Expected within 6 hours of time of issue
Soon	Expected within 6 to 12 hours of time of issue
Later	Expected more than 12 hours from time of issue

Speed of movement of pressure systems

DESCRIPTION	SPEED (KNOTS)
Slowly	Less than 15
Steadily	15–25
Quickly	25–35
Rapidly	35–45
Very rapidly	More than 45

Wind descriptions

DESCRIPTION	MEANING
Direction	Direction from which wind is blowing
Wind becoming cyclonic	Rapid change in direction usually associated with a frontal system
Veering	Wind direction changing in a clockwise direction – e.g. south-west to west
Backing	Wind direction changing in an anticlockwise direction – e.g. east to north-east

Visibility

DESCRIPTION	MEANING
Fog	Less than 1,000 metres (approx. 0.6 nautical miles)
Poor	Between 1,000 metres and 2 nautical miles
Moderate	Between 2 and 5 nautical miles
Good	More than 5 nautical miles

PADDLING IN THE BRINY has long held an appeal for the English:

What ho, Mrs Brisket,
Why not take a plunge and risk it?
The water's warm,
There ain't no crabs
And you'll have a lot of fun among the shrimps and dabs.
If for a lark
Some saucy old shark
Takes a nibble at your chocolate biscuit
Swim for the shore
And the crowd will roar
What ho, Mrs Brisket!

'What Ho, Mrs Brisket' (1963),
Noël Coward (1899–1973)

An Englishman's Home

WHILE MOST OF US LIVE in modest surroundings, there are those for whom the home is indeed a castle. Some of them are grand and stately; others rather more threatening.

Nancy Mitford took in her own childhood experiences when she wrote *The Pursuit of Love*, but acknowledged that she owed a debt to Evelyn Waugh when it came to describing the family house:

Alconleigh was a large, ugly, north-facing Georgian house, built with only one intention – that of sheltering, when the weather was too bad to be out of doors, a succession of bucolic squires, their wives, their enormous families, their dogs, their horses, their father's relict, and their unmarried sisters. There was no attempt at decoration, at softening the lines, no apology for a façade, it was all as grim and as bare as a barracks, stuck upon the high hillside. Within, the keynote, the theme, was death. Not death of maidens, not death romantically accoutred with urns and weeping willows, cypresses and valedictory odes, but death of warriors and of animals, stark, real. On the walls halberds and pikes and ancient muskets were arranged in crude patterns with the heads of beasts slaughtered in many lands, with the flags and uniforms of bygone Radletts. Glass-topped cases contained not miniatures of ladies, but miniatures of the medals of their lords, badges, penholders made of tiger's teeth, the hoof of a favourite horse, telegrams announcing casualties in battle, and commissions written out on parchment scrolls, all lying together in a timeless jumble.

The Pursuit of Love (1945),
Nancy Mitford (1904–73)

THE FASCINATION WITH THE MITFORD sisters seems to continue unabated, to the amazement of Debo, now the Dowager Duchess of Devonshire, Nancy's sister. She describes her 'office' at Chatsworth:

The cupboard is stuffed with boxes of letters to and from my family, a growing archive that is suddenly of interest and, apparently, of value, which seems so strange when it is just parents, sisters, children and friends writing to one another. They start with the diaries of my mother, in love with her skating instructor when she was seventeen (as we all were in our youth, a passion now transferred to ski guides) and spending summers on her father's ketch at Trouville in the company of the artists Helleu, Boldini and Tissot. The thousands of letters to and from my sisters, Nancy, Pam, Diana, Unity and Jessica, my brother Tom, myself, nannies and cousins might give the true picture of our upbringing. Diana's daughter-in-law, Charlotte Mosley, has the courage to tackle the piles of paper and is to edit a volume of the sisters' letters to each other.*

Television enquirers are curious about our childhood. It seemed perfectly ordinary to us, but they won't be fobbed

---

* *The Mitfords: Letters Between Six Sisters* (Fourth Estate, 2007)

off with that, so they embroider till it all sounds exciting. It is very odd to have been part of the pantomime the directors favour.

When strangers see the heaps of papers on the floor, patterns of fabrics to be used in this house and at the Devonshire Arms Hotel, at Bolton Abbey, at Lismore Castle and the holiday cottages in Wetton, carrier bags bursting with postcards, a bigger one entitled 'Letters to Keep', pictures propped against the wall, baskets with used envelopes I can't bear to throw away and dog's double beds, they find it difficult to stick to what we planned to talk about.

I admire the denizens of grand offices where the huge desk is bare but for a telephone politely cut off for the duration of the visit – but I can't imagine how that is done.

The rag rugs on the floor are my daughter Emma's winter work. Her watercolours – here of lilies, orchids and a pear – are painted in the summer.

My loved plastic lamps in the shape of ducks, owls and a sheep are dismissed as 'kitsch' by those who prefer something more expensive. Alas, the shop where I bought them has gone bust.

Chatsworth: The House (2002),
the Duchess of Devonshire (1920–)

Things No English Home Should Be Without

Scrabble
a pair of slippers
a coir doormat
an egg-poacher
a table to eat round
a log fire
a poker
Country Life
a tea tray
a teapot
a kettle
Inspector Morse on DVD
Rummikub
string
wellies
a Labrador
bookshelves
Love Actually on DVD
the *Radio Times*

eggcups

a Beatles CD

playing cards

a coal scuttle

a clock that ticks

best china

family photographs in frames

a pouffe

a frying pan

Pride and Prejudice on DVD (the BBC one)

Earl Grey and lapsang tea

an easy chair

stamps

a cat

masses of books

a Roberts wireless

napkins

a barometer

Germolene

a Tilly hat

Sense and Sensibility on DVD

a fountain pen

spare birthday cards

plimsolls

a standard lamp

The Book of Common Prayer

a diary
Price's candles
paperclips
a pencil sharpener – and pencils
Post-it Notes
coasters
Antiquax wax polish
dusters
Cherry Blossom shoe polish
The Railway Children on DVD
a shopping basket
writing paper and envelopes
fresh flowers
place mats
Swarfega
a black umbrella
a Barbour
Bleak House on DVD
Colgate toothpaste
scissors
postcards
a bicycle
and, if there's room . . .
. . . chickens.

E VELYN WAUGH HIMSELF would sit in his own miniature
stately home in Gloucestershire writing letters to the likes
of Randolph Churchill, son of Winston Churchill, bemoaning
his lot at the end of the Second World War:

TO RANDOLPH CHURCHILL

8 October 1945   Piers Court

This morning a rare and beautiful gift arrived for me. I
thank you with all my heart. The cigars would have been a
keen pleasure at any time; doubly so now for I am living in
conditions of Balkan austerity. We have no servants; Laura
broods despondently over the kitchen range and periodically
raises columns of black smoke, announces that our meat ra-
tion has been incinerated, and drives me to dinner at a neigh-
bouring inn. Most of her day is spent in cooking potatoes for
the poultry – twenty-seven hens who lay three eggs a day be-
tween them. The domestic hot-water machine has burst and
flooded the kitchen quarters. We have had no hot water for a
week. But hungry and dirty as I am, I shall now be content
for an hour a day for twenty-five days thanks to your munifi-
cence. In twenty-five days my butler will be out of the army,
the plumber will have put in a boiler, a cook may have been

found and I may be equipped to invite you to visit me.
I come to London for the day on the twenty-sixth of this month and will search White's for you.

The Letters of Evelyn Waugh (1980),
Evelyn Waugh (1903–66)

Bᴜᴛ ᴡʜᴇɴ Eᴠᴇʟʏɴ Wᴀᴜɢʜ wasn't writing letters, he was more gainfully employed with his pen. *Brideshead Revisited* was published in the same year that that letter to Randolph Churchill was written, 1945, and its imagery is especially rich.

'I have been here before,' I said; I had been there before; first with Sebastian more than twenty years ago on a cloudless day in June, when the ditches were creamy with meadowsweet and the air heavy with all the scents of summer; it was a day of peculiar splendour, and though I had been there so often, in so many moods, it was to that first visit that my heart returned on this, my latest.

That day, too, I had come not knowing my destination. It was Eights Week. Oxford – submerged now and obliterated, irrecoverable as Lyonnesse, so quickly have the waters come flooding in – Oxford, in those days, was still a city of aquatint. In her spacious and quiet streets men walked and spoke as they had done in Newman's day; her autumnal mists, her grey springtime, and the rare glory of her summer days – such as that day – when the chestnut was in flower and the bells rang out high and clear over her gables and cupolas, exhaled the soft airs of centuries of youth. It was this cloistral hush which gave our laughter its resonance, and carried it still, joyously, over the intervening clamour.

Here, discordantly, in Eights Week, came a rabble of womankind, some hundreds strong, twittering and fluttering over the cobbles and up the steps, sight-seeing and pleasure-seeking, drinking claret cup, eating cucumber sandwiches; pushed in punts about the river, herded in droves to the college barges; greeting in the Isis and in the Union by a sudden display of peculiar, facetious, wholly distressing Gilbert-and-Sullivan badinage, and by peculiar choral effects in the College chapels. Echoes of the intruders penetrated every corner, and in my own College was no echo, but an original fount of the grossest disturbance. We were giving a ball. The front quad, where I lived, was floored and tented; palms and azaleas were banked round the porter's lodge; worst of all, the don who lived above me, a mouse of a man connected with the Natural Sciences, had lent his rooms for a ladies' cloakroom, and a printed notice proclaiming this outrage hung not six inches from my oak.

No one felt more strongly about it than my scout.

'Gentlemen who haven't got ladies are asked as far as possible to take their meals out in the next few days,' he announced despondently. 'Will you be lunching in?'

'No, Lunt.'

'So as to give the servants a chance, they say. What a chance! I've got to buy a *pin-cushion* for the ladies' cloakroom. What do they want with dancing? I don't see the reason in it. There never was dancing before in Eights Week.

Commem. now is another matter being in the vacation, but not in Eights Week, as if teas and the river wasn't enough. If you ask me, sir, it's all on account of the war. It couldn't have happened but for that.' For this was 1923 and for Lunt, as for thousands of others, things could never be the same as they had been in 1914. 'Now wine in the evening,' he continued, as was his habit half in and half out of the door, 'or one or two gentlemen to luncheon, there's reason in. But not dancing. It all came in with the men back from the war. They were too old and they didn't know and they wouldn't learn. That's the truth. And there's some even goes dancing with the town at the Masonic – but the proctors will get *them*, you see ... Well, here's Lord Sebastian. I mustn't stand here talking when there's pin-cushions to get.'

Sebastian entered – dove-grey flannel, white *crêpe de Chine*, a Charvet tie, my tie as it happened, a pattern of postage stamps – 'Charles, what in the world's happening at your college? Is there a circus? I've seen everything except elephants. I must say the whole of Oxford has become *most* peculiar suddenly. Last night it was pullulating with women. You're to come away at once, out of danger. I've got a motor-car and a basket of strawberries and a bottle of Château Peyraguey – which isn't a wine you've ever tasted, so don't pretend. It's heaven with strawberries.'

Brideshead Revisited (1945), Evelyn Waugh (1903–66)

Rebecca

D APHNE DU MAURIER WAS the mistress of atmosphere. Of all the first lines in all the novels ever written, only that of *Pride and Prejudice* is on an equal footing in terms of memorability with the opening lines of *Rebecca*, published in 1938 and engraved on many a heart to this day.

Last night I dreamt I went to Manderley again. It seemed to me I stood by the iron gate leading to the drive, and for a while I could not enter, for the way was barred to me. There was a padlock and a chain upon the gate. I called in my dream to the lodge-keeper, and had no answer, and peering closer through the rusted spokes of the gate I saw that the lodge was uninhabited.

No smoke came from the chimney, and the little lattice windows gaped forlorn. Then, like all dreamers, I was possessed of a sudden with supernatural powers and passed like a spirit through the barrier before me. The drive wound away in front of me, twisting and turning as it had always done, but as I advanced I was aware that a change had come upon it; it was narrow and unkept, not the drive that we had known. At first I was puzzled and did not understand, and it was only when I bent my head to avoid the low swinging branch of a tree that I realised what had happened. Nature had come into her own again and, little by little, in her stealthy, insidious way had encroached upon the drive with long, tenacious fingers. The woods, always a menace even in the past, had triumphed in the end. They crowded, dark and uncontrolled, to the borders of the drive. The beeches with white, naked limbs leant close to one another, their branches intermingled in a strange embrace, making a vault above my head like the archway of a church. And there were other trees as well, trees that I did not recognise, squat oaks and tortured elms that straggled cheek by jowl with the beeches, and had thrust themselves out of the quiet earth, along with monster shrubs and plants, none of which I remembered.

The drive was a ribbon now, a thread of its former self, with gravel surface gone, and choked with grass and moss. The trees had thrown out low branches, making an impediment to progress; the gnarled roots looked like skeleton claws. Scattered here and again amongst this jungle growth I would recognise shrubs that had been land-marks in our time, things of culture and of grace, hydrangeas whose blue heads had been famous. No hand had checked their progress, and they had gone native now, rearing to monster height without a bloom, black and ugly as the nameless parasites that grew beside them.

On and on, now east now west, wound the poor thread that once had been our drive. Sometimes I thought it lost, but it appeared again, beneath a fallen tree perhaps, or struggling on the other side of a muddied ditch created by the winter rains. I had not thought the way so long. Surely the miles had multiplied, even as the trees had done, and this path led but to a labyrinth, some choked wilderness, and not to the house at all. I came upon it suddenly; the approach masked by the unnatural growth of a vast shrub that spread in all directions, and I stood, my heart thumping in my breast, the strange prick of tears behind my eyes.

There was Manderley, our Manderley, secretive and silent as it had always been, the grey stone shining in the moonlight of my dream, the mullioned windows reflecting the green lawns and the terrace. Time could not wreck the perfect symmetry of those walls, nor the site itself, a jewel in the hollow of a hand.

Rebecca (1938),
Daphine du Maurier (1907–89)

Bᴜᴛ ᴇɴᴏᴜɢʜ ᴏꜰ ᴛʜᴇ sɪɴɪsᴛᴇʀ, what we need is a stately home that is unthreatening; one that sits under a cloudless sky. Such a place is Blandings Castle in Shropshire, home of the Earl of Emsworth. If I can't live in *The Wind in the Willows* when I grow up, then I want to be Lord Emsworth and spend most of the day touring my demesnes and curtilages, and leaning over the sty of the Empress of Blandings and scratching her back. But there are flies, even in Lord Emsworth's ointment of life.

The day was so warm, so fair, so magically a thing of sunshine and blue skies and bird-song that anyone acquainted with Clarence, ninth Earl of Emsworth, and aware of his liking for fine weather, would have pictured him going about the place on this summer morning with a beaming smile and an uplifted heart. Instead of which, humped over the breakfast-table, he was directing at a blameless kippered herring a look of such intense bitterness that the fish seemed to sizzle beneath it. For it was August Bank Holiday, and Blandings Castle on August Bank Holiday became, in his lordship's opinion, a miniature Inferno.

This was the day when his park and grounds broke out into a noisome rash of swings, roundabouts, marquees, toy balloons and paper bags; when a tidal wave of the peasantry and its squealing young engulfed those haunts of immemorial peace. On August Bank Holiday he was not allowed to potter pleasantly about his gardens in an old coat: forces beyond his control shoved him into a stiff collar and a top hat and told him to go out and be genial. And in the cool of the quiet evenfall they put him on a platform and made him make a speech. To a man with a day like that in front of him fine weather was a mockery.

His sister, Lady Constance Keeble, looked brightly at him over the coffee-pot.

'What a lovely morning!' she said.

Lord Emsworth's gloom deepened. He chafed at being called upon – by this woman of all others – to behave as if everything was for the jolliest in the jolliest of all possible worlds. But for his sister, Constance, and her hawk-like vigilance, he might, he thought, have been able at least to dodge the top-hat.

'Have you got your speech ready?'

'Yes.'

'Well, mind you learn it by heart this time and don't stammer and dodder as you did last year.'

Lord Emsworth pushed plate and kipper away. He had lost his desire for food.

'And don't forget you have to go to the village this morning to judge the cottage gardens.'

'All right, all right, all right,' said his lordship testily. 'I've not forgotten.'

'I think I will come to the village with you. There are a number of those Fresh Air London children staying there now, and I must warn them to behave properly when they come to the fête this afternoon. You know what London children are. McAllister says he found one of them in the gardens the other day, picking his flowers.'

At any other time the news of this outrage would, no doubt, have affected Lord Emsworth profoundly. But now, so intense was his self-pity, he did not even shudder. He drank coffee with the air of a man who regretted that it was not hemlock.

'By the way, McAllister was speaking to me again last night about that gravel path through the yew alley. He seems very keen on it.'

'Glug!' said Lord Emsworth – which, as any philologist will tell you, is the sound which peers of the realm make when stricken to the soul while drinking coffee.

Concerning Glasgow, that great commercial and manufacturing city in the county of Lanarkshire in Scotland, much has been written. So lyrically does the *Encyclopaedia Britannica* deal with the place that it covers twenty-seven pages before it can tear itself away and go on to Glass, Glastonbury, Glatz and Glauber. The only aspect of it, however, which immediately concerns the present historian is the fact that the citizens it breeds are apt to be grim, dour, persevering, tenacious men; men with red whiskers who know what they

want and mean to get it. Such a one was Angus McAllister,
head-gardener at Blandings Castle.

'Lord Emsworth and the Girl Friend', *Blandings Castle* (1935),
P. G. Wodehouse (1881–1975)

W<small>HAT</small> L<small>ORD</small> E<small>MSWORTH</small> <small>NEEDED</small> was Wodehouse's other creation, Jeeves – Bertie Wooster's gentleman's gentleman. With Jeeves at his side he would have had no cause to worry, and there would have been upon his lips a carefree smile and in his heart the fluttering spirit that denotes … Well, you know the sort of thing.

I marmaladed a slice of toast with something of a flourish, and I don't suppose I have ever come much closer to saying 'Tra-la-la' as I did the lathering, for I was feeling in mid-season form this morning. God, as I once heard Jeeves put it, was in His Heaven and all right with the world. (He added, I remember, some guff about larks and snails, but that is a side issue and need not detain us.)

It is no secret in the circles in which he moves that Bertram Wooster, though as glamorous as one could wish when night has fallen and the revels get under way, is seldom a ball of fire at the breakfast table. Confronted with the eggs and b., he tends to pick cautiously at them, as if afraid they may leap from the plate and snap at him. Listless, about sums it up. Not much bounce to the ounce.

But today vastly different conditions had prevailed. All had been verve, if that's the word I want, and animation. Well, when I tell you that after sailing through a couple of sausages like a tiger of the jungle tucking into its luncheon coolie, I was now, as indicated, about to tackle the toast and marmalade, I fancy I need say no more.

The reason for this improved outlook on the proteins and carbohydrates is not far to seek. Jeeves was back, earning his weekly envelope once more at the old stand. Her butler having come down with an ailment of some sort, my Aunt Dahlia, my good and deserving aunt, had borrowed him for a house-party she was throwing at Brinkley Court, her Worcester-shire residence, and he had been away for more than a week. Jeeves, of course, is a gentleman's gentleman, not a butler, but if the call comes, he can buttle with the best of them. It's in the blood. His Uncle Charlie is a butler, and no doubt he has picked up many a hint on technique from him.

Stiff Upper Lip, Jeeves (1963),
P. G. Wodehouse (1881–1975)

Lord Elderley, Lord Borrowmere,
Lord Sickert and Lord Camp
With every virtue, every grace,
Ah what avails the sceptred race,
Here you see – the four of us,
And there are so many more of us,
Eldest sons that must succeed.
We know how Caesar conquered Gaul
And how to whack a cricket ball;
Apart from this, our education
Lacks co-ordination.
Though we're young and tentative,
And rather rip-representative,
Scions of a noble breed,
We are the products of those homes serene and stately
Which only lately
Seem to have run to seed!

The stately homes of England,
How beautiful they stand,
To prove the upper classes
Have still the upper hand;

An Englishman's Home

Though the fact that they have to be rebuilt
And frequently mortgaged to the hilt
Is inclined to take the gilt
Off the gingerbread,
And certainly damps the fun
Of the eldest son –
But still we won't be beaten,
We'll scrimp and scrape and save,
The playing-fields of Eton
Have made us frightfully brave –
And though if the Van Dycks have to go
And we pawn the Bechstein grand,
We'll stand
By the stately homes of England.

Here you see
The pick of us,
You may be heartily sick of us,
Still with sense
We're all imbued.
Our homes command extensive views
And with assistance from the Jews
We have been able to dispose of
Rows and rows and rows of
Gainsboroughs and Lawrences,
Some sporting prints of Aunt Florence's,

Some of which were rather rude.
Although we sometimes flaunt our family conventions,
Our good intentions
Mustn't be misconstrued.

The stately homes of England
We proudly represent,
We only keep them up for Americans to rent.
Though the pipes that supply the bathroom burst
And the lavatory makes you fear the worst,
It was used by Charles the First,
Quite informally,
And later by George the Fourth
On a journey north.
The state apartments keep their
Historical renown,
It's wiser not to sleep there
In case they tumble down;
But still if they ever catch on fire
Which, with any luck, they might
We'll fight
For the stately homes of England.

The stately homes of England,
Though rather in the lurch,
Provide a lot of chances

An Englishman's Home

For Psychical Research –
There's the ghost of a crazy younger son
Who murdered, in thirteen fifty-one,
An extremely rowdy nun
Who resented it,
And people who come to call
Meet her in the hall.
The baby in the guest wing,
Who crouches by the grate,
Was walled up in the west wing
In fourteen twenty-eight.
If anyone spots
The Queen of Scots
In a hand-embroidered shroud
We're proud
Of the stately homes of England.

Lord Elderley, Lord Borrowmere,
Lord Sickert and Lord Camp,
Behold us in our hours of ease,
Uncertain, coy and hard to please.
Reading in Debrett of us,
This fine patrician quartette of us,
We can feel extremely proud,
Our ancient lineage we trace
Back to the cradle of the race

Before those beastly Roman bowmen
Bitched our local yeomen.
Though our new democracy
May pain the old aristocracy
We've not winced nor cried aloud,
Under the bludgeonings of chance,
What will be – will be.
Our heads will still be
Bloody but quite unbowed!

The stately homes of England,
Although a trifle bleak,
Historically speaking,
Are more or less unique.
We've a cousin who won the Golden Fleece
And a very peculiar fowling-piece
Which was sent to Cromwell's niece,
Who detested it,
And rapidly sent it back
With a dirty crack.
A note we have from Chaucer
Contains a bawdy joke.
We also have a saucer
That Bloody Mary broke.
We've two pairs of tights
King Arthur's Knights

Had completely worn away.
Sing Hey!
For the stately homes of England!

The stately homes of England,
Tho' rather on the blink
Provide a lot of reasons
For what we do and think.
Tho' we freely admit we may be wrong,
Our conviction that we are right is strong,
Tho' it may not be for long,
We'll hold on to it.
We might as well hold the bat
Till they knock us flat.
Our dignity of race may
Retire into its shell,
Our Minister of Grace may
Defend us none too well,
But still if a child
Becomes too wild
And we're forced to use the rod,
Thank God
For the stately homes of England

'The Stately Homes of England' (1938),
Noël Coward (1899–1973)

Bᴜᴛ ᴘᴇʀʜᴀᴘs ᴡᴇ sʜᴏᴜʟᴅ not pine for the life of the
gentry. On the surface all may seem plain sailing, and yet
beneath the well-mannered veneer ...

The Countess of Coteley!
Wife of the Eleventh Earl,
Mother of four fine children,
Three boys and a girl.
Coteley Park in Sussex,
Strathrar on the Dee,
Palace Gardens, Kensington,
Aged thirty-three.

Look at the Countess of Coteley!
Here you see her when
She was at her zenith and the year was nineteen ten.

Is she happy, would you guess?
The answer to that question is, more or less.

For she's never heard of Hitler, and she's never thought of war,
She's got twenty-seven servants, and she could get twenty more.
She never sees a paper, and she seldom reads a book,
She is worshipped by her butler, tolerated by her cook.

And her husband treats her nicely, and he's *mostly* on a horse,
While the children are entirely in the nursery of course.
So no wonder she is happy – she's got nothing else to do.
O, no wonder she is happy, for she hasn't got a clue,
To the future that is waiting, and the funny things she'll do
About … thirty-seven years from now.

When you see her in this flashback it is rather hard to guess
That she'll be a sort of typist in the W.V.S.
She will learn to woo her grocer: she won't have a cook to woo,
But a Czechoslovak cleaner may pop in from twelve to two.
Speaking worldlily she'll dwindle. She will change her book
at Boots,
And lecture on Make-Do-and-Mend to Women's Institutes.
She will lose the Earl quite quietly, and her young will leave the
    nest,
She never knew them very well, so that is for the best.
And Coteley, Strathrar, Kensington will vanish with the rest
About … thirty-seven years from now.

Now the National Trust has Coteley, which is quite a handy
    dodge,
And she'll make a flat of part of what was once the keeper's lodge.
She will seldom dress for dinner, she will dote on Vera Lynn,
She will take in the *New Statesman*, but she won't be taken in.

England, Our England

Here you see her in this flashback looking decorative but dumb,
For she hasn't got an inkling of the jolly days to come!
Though the distances she'll travel are incredible to tell,
And the quandaries she'll cope with will be absolutely hell,
She'll emerge in forty-seven having done it rather well!

Will she be happy, would you guess?
The answer to that is … y-e-s.

'The Countess of Coteley' (1978),
Joyce Grenfell (1910–79)

Our England
Is a Garden

IT IS NO IDLE BOAST TO SAY that England's gardens are the finest in the world. The monks in the monasteries created our first gardens, and our early sailors brought back plants from foreign climes to enrich our native flora. The Tudor monarchs saw gardens as a way of expressing their power – packed with rare plants and symbols of chivalry. Later kings and queens brought back from abroad not only more plants but ideas on garden design – notably Charles II from his exile in France and William III and Mary II when they moved here from Holland. The Victorian era saw the fashion for plant-collecting explode and our gardens became repositories for the exotic, the elaborate and the extravagant. Our horticultural, botanical and design expertise has been refined over five hundred years because we liked what we saw over the water and we brought it home.

The English garden as we think of it now has evolved into its present form, and no one sums it up better than Rudyard Kipling:

Our England is a garden that is full of stately views,
Of borders, beds and shrubberies and lawns and avenues,
With statues on the terraces and peacocks strutting by;

England, Our England

But the Glory of the Garden lies in more than meets the eye.
For where the old thick laurels grow, along the thin red wall,
You find the tool- and potting-sheds which are the heart of all;
The cold-frames and the hot-houses, the dungpits and the tanks,
The rollers, carts and drain-pipes, with the barrows and the
planks.

And there you'll see the gardeners, the man and 'prentice boys
Told off to do as they are bid and do it without noise;
For, except when seeds are planted and we shout to scare the
   birds,
The Glory of the Garden it abideth not in words.

And some can pot begonias and some can bud a rose,
And some are hardly fit to trust with anything that grows;
But they can roll and trim the lawns and sift the sand and loam,
For the Glory of the Garden occupieth all who come.

Our England is a garden, and such gardens are not made
By singing:– 'Oh, how beautiful!' and sitting in the shade,
While better men than we go out and start their working lives
At grubbing weeds from gravel-paths with broken dinner-knives.

There's not a pair of legs so thin, there's not a head so thick,
There's not a hand so weak and white, nor yet a heart so sick,

Our England Is a Garden

But it can find some needful job that's crying to be done,
For the Glory of the Garden glorifieth every one.

Then seek your job with thankfulness and work till further
    orders,
If it's only netting strawberries or killing slugs on borders;
And when your back stops aching and your hands begin to
    harden,
You will find yourself a partner in the Glory of the Garden.

Oh, Adam was a gardener, and God who made him sees
That half a proper gardener's work is done upon his knees,
So when your work is finished, you can wash your hands and
    pray
For the Glory of the Garden, that it may not pass away!
And the Glory of the Garden it shall never pass away!

'The Glory of the Garden' (1911),
Rudyard Kipling (1865–1936)

M Y FIRST GARDENING BOOK? I remember it vividly. And the opening lines:

Flopsy, Mopsy and Cottontail, who were good little bunnies, went down the lane to gather blackberries: but Peter, who was very naughty, ran straight away to Mr McGregor's garden and squeezed under the gate!

First he ate some lettuces and some French beans; and then he ate some radishes; and then, feeling rather sick, he went to look for some parsley.

But round the end of a cucumber frame, whom should he meet but Mr McGregor!

Mr McGregor was on his hands and knees planting out young cabbages, but he jumped up and ran after Peter, waving a rake and calling out, 'Stop, thief!'

The Tale of Peter Rabbit (1901),
Beatrix Potter (1866–1943)

A ND THE SECOND ONE:

The Mole struck a match, and by its light the Rat saw that they were standing in an open space, neatly swept and sanded underfoot, and directly facing them was Mole's little front door, with 'Mole End' painted, in Gothic lettering, over the bell-pull at the side.

Mole reached down a lantern from a nail on the wall and lit it, and the Rat, looking round him, saw that they were in a sort of fore-court. A garden seat stood on one side of the door, and on the other a roller; for the Mole, who was a tidy animal when at home, could not stand having his ground kicked up by other animals into little runs that ended in earth heaps. On the walls hung wire baskets with ferns in them, alternating with brackets carrying plaster statuary – Garibaldi, and the infant Samuel, and Queen Victoria, and other heroes of modern Italy. Down one side of the fore-court ran a skittle-alley, with benches along it and little wooden tables marked with rings that hinted at beer mugs. In the middle was a small round pond containing goldfish and surrounded by a cockle-shell border. Out of the centre of the pond rose a fanciful erection clothed in more cockle-shells and topped by a large silvered glass ball that reflected everything all wrong and had a very pleasing effect.

The Wind in the Willows (1908), Kenneth Grahame (1859–1932)

THE THIRD ONE, I found a bit scary:

A large rose-tree stood near the entrance of the garden: the roses growing on it were white, but there were three gardeners at it, busily painting them red. Alice thought this a very curious thing, and she went nearer to watch them, and just as she came up to them she heard one of them say, 'Look out now, Five! Don't go splashing paint over me like that!'

'I couldn't help it,' said Five, in a sulky tone. 'Seven jogged my elbow.'

On which Seven looked up and said, 'That's right, Five! Always lay the blame on others!'

'*You'd* better not talk!' said Five. 'I heard the Queen say only yesterday you deserved to be beheaded!'

'What for?' said the one who had first spoken.

'That's none of *your* business, Two!' said Seven.

'Yes, it *is* his business!' said Five. 'And I'll tell him – it was for bringing the cook tulip roots instead of onions.'

Seven flung down his brush, and had just begun 'Well, of all the unjust things—' when his eye chanced to fall upon Alice, as she stood watching them, and he checked himself suddenly: the others looked round also, and all of them bowed low.

'Would you tell me,' said Alice, a little timidly, 'why you are painting those roses?'

Five and Seven said nothing, but looked at Two. Two began in a low voice, 'Why, the fact is, you see, Miss, this here ought to have been a *red* rose-tree, and we put a white one in by mistake; and if the Queen was to find it out, we should have our heads cut off, you know. So you see, Miss, we're doing our best, afore she comes, to—' At this moment, Five, who had been anxiously looking across the garden, called out, 'The Queen! The Queen!' and the three gardeners instantly threw themselves flat upon their faces. There was a sound of many footsteps, and Alice looked round, eager to see the Queen.

Alice's Adventures in Wonderland (1865),
Lewis Carroll (1832–98)

The Best-Scented Shrub Roses

'Belle de Crécy'
'Celestial'
'Charles de Mills'
'Conrad Ferdinand Meyer'
'Empress Josephine'
'Fantin-Latour'
'Général Kléber'
'Gloire des Mousseux'
'Hugh Dickson'
'Konigin von Danemark'
'Louise Odier'
'Maiden's Blush'
'Madame Hardy'
'Madame Isaac Pereire'
'Reine des Violettes'
'Rose à Parfum de l'Hay'
'Roseraie de l'Hay'
'Souvenir de la Malmaison'

'Tis odd, but very true indeed,
A gardener does not grow from seed;
Nor from a bulb; nor from a shoot
Cut from a well-developed root.

His slow beginnings, who can trace?
He springs from a peculiar race.
The child of hope and second sight,
Born of despair and of delight.

Nursed by uncertainties and guesses;
Nourished by failures and successes;
From ceaseless toil in sun and shade
He is evolved – but never made.

'How Does a Gardener Grow?' (date unknown),
Fay Inchfawn (1881–unknown)

BEING A BIT OF A SLOW starter at school, I should have found Shakespeare beyond me, but the first play we did was *A Midsummer Night's Dream* and I was hooked – especially by Puck's speech:

> I know a bank where the wild thyme blows,
> Where oxlips and the nodding violet grows;
> Quite over-canopied with luscious woodbine,
> With sweet musk-roses, and with eglantine:
> There sleeps Titania sometime of the night,
> Lull'd in these flowers with dances and delight . . .

A Midsummer Night's Dream (1595–96), Act II, Scene 1,
William Shakespeare (1564–1616)

Our England Is a Garden

I WAS LUCKY ENOUGH TO be able to grow things. From about the age of eight. It was never difficult. Well, there were always a few plants that were tricky, but that was part of the challenge. Looking after most things – and sowing seeds and taking cuttings – felt completely natural. Later on I found that Laurie Lee summed it up nicely:

> Mother's father had a touch with horses; she had the same with flowers. She could grow them anywhere, at any time, and they seemed to live longer for her. She grew them with rough, almost slap-dash love, but her hands possessed such an understanding of their needs they seemed to turn to her like another sun. She could snatch a dry root from field or hedgerow, dab it into the garden, give it a shake – and almost immediately it flowered. One felt she could grow roses from a stick or chair-leg, so remarkable was this gift.

Cider With Rosie (1959),
Laurie Lee (1914–97)

I DECIDED AT THE AGE OF ten that I would become a gardener, and at fifteen I left school and went to work in the local Parks Department nursery in Ilkley, Yorkshire. My first day's work was eventful enough – being given my own greenhouses to look after – but it had nothing on that of Sir Joseph Paxton, designer of the Crystal Palace, who became the Duke of Devonshire's head gardener at Chatsworth. He was working in Chiswick at the time and had to make the long journey north:

> I left London by the Comet coach for Chesterfield, arrived at Chatsworth at half past four o'clock in the morning of the ninth of May, 1826. As no person was to be seen at that early hour, I got over the greenhouse gate by the old covered way, explored the pleasure grounds, and looked round the outside of the house. I then went down to the kitchen gardens, scaled the outside wall, and saw the whole of the place, set the men to work there at six o'clock; then returned to Chatsworth, and got Thomas Weldon to play me the waterworks, and afterwards went to breakfast with poor dear Mrs Gregory and her niece: the latter fell in love with me, and I with her, and thus completed my first morning's work at Chatsworth before nine o'clock.

Sir Joseph Paxton (1801–65)

Some of England's Best Gardens

Alnwick Castle, Northumberland

Home of the Duke and Duchess of Northumberland, this is a great garden for families (children are encouraged to drive mini-diggers at the foot of the cascade!) – water cascades and fountains, the largest treehouse in the world, a poison garden, a bamboo labyrinth and plenty of flowers.

Beth Chatto Gardens, Essex

Created by England's best-loved female gardener, this rolling landscape shows how all kinds of plants can be grown to best effect – often in difficult situations. There are dry and gravel gardens, a woodland garden and water gardens. Inspirational.

Chatsworth, Derbyshire

Home of the Duke and Duchess of Devonshire – a wonderful 'Capability' Brown landscape as well as the Emperor Fountain, the Great Cascade, the peaches and camellias on the

Conservative Wall, plus flower borders, woodland walks, a maze, a kitchen garden, trees – the list goes on.

The Garden House, Devon

Inspirational use of plants and tremendous views of Dartmoor. Cottage gardens, a quarry garden and a flower-filled meadow that will send you into ecstasies in late spring and early summer.

Great Dixter Gardens, East Sussex

The late Christopher Lloyd's garden is one for the plantsman and garden lover alike – plants are grown in striking combinations. Ancient topiary, stunning long borders and a tropical garden that will make you smile.

Hidcote Manor Garden, Gloucestershire

Created by the late Major Lawrence Johnston in the early part of the twentieth century, Hidcote is the original 'garden of rooms' and still brilliant today. Look for the Red Borders – hot on the dullest of days.

Kew Gardens, Surrey

The world's leading botanic garden and a great day out. Woodland walks, Decimus Burton's great Palm House and masses of other greenhouses filled with exotic plants (the Princess of Wales Conservatory is particularly spectacular), as well as Kew Palace (once home to King George III), the Pagoda (now open to the public) and the massive Temperate House.

Rousham Manor, Oxfordshire

A sublime eighteenth-century landscape created by William Kent. Full of temples, a rolling main of clipped laurel that positively sparkles under the trees (dull it ain't), canals and watercourses and Arcadian views all arranged around a handsome manor house.

Sissinghurst Castle Garden, Kent

Created by Vita Sackville-West and Sir Harold Nicolson, Sissinghurst is a gem of a garden with its Elizabethan tower, interlocking vistas, connecting garden rooms (inspired by Hidcote) and its famous White Garden.

Stourhead, Wiltshire

Henry Hoare's eighteenth-century Arcadian landscape – a breathtaking confection of bridges and temples, views and vistas, follies and trees, all reflected in a shimmering lake. Staggeringly beautiful.

Stowe Landscape Gardens, Buckinghamshire

'Capability' Brown's masterpiece – a landscape sculpted as only Brown knew how, and decorated with a generous supply of temples and follies. A sublime piece of classical English countryside.

Studley Royal, Yorkshire

Created by Georgian politician John Aislabie, this is perhaps England's most sublime landscape garden – a series of dramatic water features and temples culminate in a view of Fountains Abbey at the end of the valley. Matchless.

Tresco Abbey Garden, Isles of Scilly

You'd think you were in the Mediterranean. Lush plantings of exotic and tender plants (over 20,000 of them from 80 countries) in a wonderful setting – a jewel of an island surrounded by turquoise sea. (Well, most days, anyway.)

Our England Is a Garden

Blessed are the botanists, for they shall inherit a rich, fibrous loam.

Cyril Connolly (1903–74)

TENNYSON IS AN ACQUIRED taste. I wish I loved him more. Joyce Grenfell is more my bag. You can guess for yourself who wrote which bits:

Come into the garden, Maud,
For the black bat, night, has flown,
Come into the garden, Maud,
I am here at the gate alone.
And the woodbine spices are wafted abroad,
And the musk of the rose is blown.

Maud won't come into the garden,
Maud is compelled to state,
Though you stand for hours in among the flowers,
Down by the garden gate.
Maud won't come into the garden,
Sing to her as you may.
Maud says she begs your pardon,
But she wasn't born yesterday.

She is coming, my love, my dear,
She is coming, my life, my fate,
The red rose cries 'She is near, she is near',
And the white rose cries 'She is late!'

Our England Is a Garden

But Maud's not coming into the garden
Thanking you just the same,
Though she looks so pure, you may be quite sure,
Maud's on to your little game.
Maud knows how she's being damping,
And how damp you already must be,
So Maudie is now decamping,
To her lovely hot-water B.

Come into the garden, Maud ...
Frankly, Maud wouldn't dream of coming into the garden,
Let that be understood,
When the nights are warm, Maud knows the form,
Maud has read 'Red Riding Hood'.
Maud did not need much warning,
She'd watched you with those pink gins,
So she bids you a kind 'good morning',
And advises two aspirins.

Maud ...

You couldn't really seriously think that Maud was going to be
    such a sucker as to come into the garden,
Flowers set her teeth on edge,
And she's much too old for a strangle-hold in a prickly privet
    hedge.

Pray stand till your arteries harden,
It won't do the slightest good.
Maud is not coming into the garden,
And you're mad to have thought she would!

'Come Into the Garden, Maud',
Joyce Grenfell (1910–79) and
'Maud' (1855),
Alfred, Lord Tennyson (1809–92)

Famous English Gardeners

Lancelot 'Capability' Brown (1716–83)

England's most famous landscape gardener, born at Kirkharle, Northumberland, and famous for his work at Bowood House, Chatsworth, Stowe, Longleat and many other country estates. He aimed to improve on nature. And much of the time he did.

Humphry Repton (1752–1818)

Landscape gardener born at Bury St Edmunds, Suffolk. Took over where Brown left off and produced his 'Red Books', which, with the aid of cut-outs, showed his clients how their landscapes could be transformed. He created designs for Woburn Abbey, Sheringham Park, Langley Park, Uppark and Endsleigh House in Devon, among others.

William Robinson (1838–1935)

Landscape gardener and writer born in Ireland but who spent most of his life in England and had a huge influence on gardening styles and techniques. His book *The English Flower Garden* advocated a more natural style of gardening – and that a garden should seem to grow out of its own landscape. He was a great champion of wild flowers. He influenced and became a friend of Gertrude Jekyll.

Gertrude Jekyll (1843–1932)

Garden designer, artist and writer, born in London, who worked with the architect Sir Edwin Lutyens, designing many gardens for his houses. Famous for her own garden at Munstead Wood in Surrey, her colour scheming and her advocacy of creating borders for particular seasons, expounded in *Colour in the Flower Garden*. She designed over 300 gardens – many of them in Surrey and many of them quite small.

Vita Sackville-West (1892–1962)

Writer and poet married to diplomat Sir Harold Nicolson (the design half of the gardening partnership), Vita Sackville-West is now most famous for her creation at Sissinghurst in Kent – around an ancient castellated house and tower. Her writings in the *Observer* from 1946–61 were devoured by the gardening cognoscenti, and her White Garden is famed throughout the world.

Sir Geoffrey Jellicoe (1900–96)

Influential architect, town planner and landscape architect who worked with Russell Page and went on to design gardens for many houses, including Sandringham, Ditchley Park, Chequers and

Chevening, and for Hemel Hempstead New Town, Plymouth Civic Centre and the Kennedy Memorial at Runnymede, Berkshire.

Russell Page (1906–85)

Landscape and garden designer who set up in partnership with Geoffrey Jellicoe in 1928. Designed gardens all over the world as well as at Charterhouse School (where he was educated) and Royal Lodge, Windsor. Most famous for his book *The Education of a Gardener*, in which he set out his theories of landscape design and planting.

Graham Stuart Thomas (1909–2003)

Botanical artist, author and gardens adviser to the National Trust, Graham Thomas is best remembered for his books, especially those on shrub roses. He championed them in *The Old Shrub Roses*, *Shrub Roses of Today* and *Climbing Roses Old and New*. His *Perennial Garden Plants* remains a source of inspiration.

Percy Thrower (1913–88)

The first television gardener, born in Buckinghamshire and eventually settling in Shrewsbury, where he became parks superintendent. Hugely influential in the 1960s and 1970s with *Gardening Club* and *Gardeners' World* on BBC Television. Percy's avuncular manner, all-round gardening knowledge and engaging style of presenting made him a household name.

Christopher Lloyd (1921–2006)

Gardener and writer born at Great Dixter in East Sussex, a garden created by his father, Nathaniel Lloyd, who wrote the standard work on topiary, *Garden Craftsmanship in Yew and Box*. Lloyd was hugely influenced by his mother, Daisy, but went on to have his own unique influence on English gardening with his brave colour combinations and well-informed but waspish style of writing. His *Well-Tempered Garden* should be on every gardener's bookshelf.

Beth Chatto (1923–)

Gardener, writer and plantswoman whose garden and nursery in Essex have become a Mecca for those who want to see plants growing in situations that suit them. Beth Chatto's knowledge of plants and their requirements is matched by her ability to create striking plant associations, and her books *The Dry Garden* and *The Damp Garden* have become classics.

HRH the Prince of Wales (1948–)

Through his garden at Highgrove (run on organic principles and open by appointment to visiting organisations), his passionate promotion of organic gardening and his books about the High-grove garden and estate, the Prince of Wales has become an in-fluential voice in recent years. The garden is a delight and the man himself an inspiration. Good on him.

'CAPABILITY' BROWN DESERVES a little more praise. It comes from the Right Hon. Charles, Lord Viscount Irwin, and was written in 1767. His lordship was clearly a fan:

> But your great Artist, like the source of light,
> Gilds every scene with beauty and delight;
> At Blenheim, Croome and Caversham we trace
> Salvator's wilderness, Claud's enlivening grace,
> Cascades and Lakes as fine as Risdale drew,
> While Nature's vary'd in each charming view.
> To paint his works would Poussin's Powers require,
> Milton's sublimity and Dryden's fire:
> For both the Sister Arts in him combin'd,
> Enrich the great ideas of his mind;
> And these still brighten all his vast designs
> For here the Painter, there the Poet shines!
> With just contempt he spurns all former rules,
> And shows true taste is not confined to schools.
> He barren tracts with every charm illumes,
> At his command a new creation blooms;
> Born to grace Nature and her works complete,
> With all that's beautiful, sublime and great!
> For him each Muse enwreaths the Laurel Crown,
> And consecrates to fame immortal Brown.

English Garden Essentials

No English garden worthy of the name should be without:

a summerhouse
a stream (natural) or rill (artificial) or, better still,
a formal canal
clipped box and yew hedges
old-fashioned shrub roses such as 'Charles de Mills' and
'Rosa Mundi'
penstemons
Geranium x riversleaianum 'Mavis Simpson'
hollyhocks
rusted ironwork fashioned into plant supports or arbours
a swing seat
a William Pye water feature (if you have the wherewithal)
a Barry Flanagan sculpture (if you have offshore accounts)
a proper lawn, with stripes
delphiniums – blue and white, rather than insipid pink
hollies
camellias in tubs (on chalk) or in woodland
(in Cornwall and Surrey)

Our England Is a Garden

a terrace (*not* a patio)
hostas (with holes in – we are organic)
hellebores
Cerinthe major 'Purpurascens'
honeysuckle

clematis
verbascums
pinks
lady's mantle
Jacob's ladder
viburnums
a greenhouse – the older the better
epimediums
ivies
old Lloyd Loom furniture
snakeshead fritillaries
peonies
a wheelbarrow
tulips
daffodils and narcissi (but not the top-heavy
'cooking' daffs)
camassias
snowdrops

mixed country hedges of hawthorn, holly,
blackthorn and briar
cardoons
cosmos
nasturtiums
pot marigolds
aubrieta

alyssum
sweet peas
a kitchen garden (however small)
an apple tree
strawberries
an asparagus bed
an *allée* of pleached hornbeams or limes
Nicotiana sylvestris
terracotta pots and urns
old and lichen-encrusted statuary
a gazebo
a washing line

THE PROSPECT OF GROWING things to eat wakes up the hunter-gatherer instinct in the mildest and most sedentary of gardeners. Added to this, the growing of vegetables in rows satisfies that deep-seated inner need for orderliness. What we need is nature's bounty, tamed. Daniel Pettiward knows what I mean:

> I want a kitchen garden
> With box to line the routes,
> Where things go soft and harden
> And cling to people's boots;
> I want dark earth to dibble
> And Brussels sprouts in droves
> And hazy days to nibble
> Among the gooseberry groves.
>
> I want to be imprisoned
> By peach-pervaded wall,
> With Quarendens wind-wizened
> And beet at beck and call,
> With marrows growing grosser
> And pumpkins past their prime
> And gardeners saying 'No, sir,'
> And 'Yes, sir,' all the time.

England, Our England

I want to be surrounded
By bone manure and bees,
With broccoli unbounded
And rhubarb to the knees,
With spinach in the making
And onions up in bed
And pippin blossom breaking
Into the potting shed.

I want to have peas podded
And cabbages neatly patched;
I want my figs home-prodded,
My apricots attached;
I want plums free from custard
And leisure to express
Myself with more than mustard
And, if it's coming, cress.

Daniel Pettiward (1913–)

Our England Is a Garden

AS A SO-CALLED GARDENING EXPERT, I am from time to time bewildered by questions which are impossible to answer. In such times of stress I am heartened by something H. E. Bates once said:

> Gardening, like love, is a funny thing, and doesn't always yield to analysis.

H. E. Bates (1905–74)

B UT MY EMBARRASSMENT at having to admit to failure is as naught compared with that of Wilfrid Blunt:

The danger of what the publication of ill-considered enthusiasm may lead to was very forcibly brought home to me when, long ago now, for a year or two I ran the gardening column in the *Sunday Times*. One October I had extolled the beauty of *Tulipa fosteriana* and recommended, with a journalist's gush, its immediate purchase and planting on a massive scale: 'If you can only afford a dozen, then buy a dozen. If you can afford a hundred, buy a hundred. But if you can afford a thousand, when May comes you will bless me.' I had myself bought, for my cat-run at Eton, half a dozen bulbs, one of which was to forget to put in an appearance. So I was not a little embarrassed when in the following spring the secretary of an Essex ladies' gardening club announced her intention of bringing two coachloads of its members to see my tulips at the height of their glory.

Wilfrid Blunt (1901–87)

PERHAPS HE SHOULD have got a man in …

There are only a few old-fashioned private gardeners left, whom everyone squabbles over, and in a few years there will be none. I don't want one. I don't want a little old man nestling in the cottage grumbling all the time. For the likes of us, the intellectual poor, all that feudal bit is finished. And I don't want an old-age pensioner lacerating the shrubs with a billhook. They ruin everything. I want to work with young people. I wouldn't mind an off-beat youth with long hair if I could get one.

Sir Roy Strong (1935–)

PLANTS AND FLOWERS AND FRUITS and vegetables have one big drawback – they catch things. They are martyrs to bugs and blights. We wish they weren't, but they are, and the list of ailments from which they suffer is likely to put off all but the keenest of cultivators. Take cucumbers. You'd like to grow some? All right, let's look them up in the book:

Greenhouse cucumbers are a delicate crop, and a host of bacterial and fungal infections can attack them. Most of these arise through incorrect soil preparation or careless management of the growing plants […] Outdoor cucumbers and marrows are much simpler to grow and are generally trouble-free, although slugs, grey mould, powdery mildew and cucumber mosaic virus can cause serious losses.

The Vegetable and Herb Expert,
Dr D. G. Hessayon

O F COURSE, YOU REALLY OUGHT to be an organic gardener and deny yourself any recourse to chemicals. You know that. I know that. But Professor John Carey still struggles to find anything in a bottle that will solve his problems:

Unfortunately the strongest and most effective ones keep being withdrawn from the market on the grounds that they have been found to damage the environment. So when you hit on a really lethal sort it's a good plan to buy it in large supply, which will allow you to go on using it after it has been outlawed. I did this for several seasons with a splendid product, now alas unobtainable, which wiped out everything from snails to flea beetles. It had no adverse effect on the bird population so far as I could see, though the neighbourhood cats did start to look a bit seedy.

That, of course, was an advantage from my point of view, for cats are filthy, insanitary beasts, and a fearful nuisance to the gardener. One of the anomalies of English law is that whereas it would, as I understand it, be an offence to clamber over your neighbour's fence and defecate among his vegetables, you can send a feline accomplice on precisely the same errand with total impunity. It has always amazed me that manufacturers of slug bait, and other such garden aids, should proudly announce on the label that their product is 'harmless to pets'. A pesticide that could guarantee to cause pets irreparable damage would, I'd have thought, sell like hot cakes.

Professor John Carey (1934–)

B<small>UT EVEN THE MOST</small> cynical – like Bernard Levin – can be converted to good garden practice in the end. He once opined:

> My view of the countryside has always been that it would be better for an ample covering of asphalt, and of flowers that they are things found in florist's for giving to pretty ladies.
>
> Bernard Levin (1928–2004)

He was eventually won over:

> Should you happen to come across me in the near future and hear me muttering things like 'Sheep nesting high this year, 'twill be a hard winter', or 'Blossom on bough, go milk a cow', or 'I don't hold wi' all this manure on the land – 'tis against nature. Give me Fison's every time', please evince no surprise. The fact is, I have acquired a windowbox and gone spectacularly horticultural overnight.

But the last word belongs to Fay Inchfawn:

> When my back is too old to bend;
> When my knees are too old to kneel;
> When my hands are too old to tend
> And fingers far too old to feel;
> When my ears will not hear again
> Leaves moving, nor the sound of rain;
> When my eyes are too old to see
> The apple orchard's ecstasy,
> O Memory!
> Stay young with me.

Fay Inchfawn (1881–unknown)

English Fare

*English cuisine is generally so threadbare that for
years there has been a gentlemen's agreement in the
civilised world to allow the Brits pre-eminence in the
matter of tea — which, after all, comes down to little
more than the ability to boil water.*

Wilfrid Sheed (1930–)

Well, that just shows how much he knows. If only it were that
straightforward.

The Perfect Cup of Tea

To make the perfect cup of tea you must:

1. Fill an empty kettle with fresh water from the tap.
2. Bring it to the boil.
3. Pour a small quantity into the teapot, which should be, in order
   of preference:

a) silver

b) EPNS

c) steel

d) china.

4. Swill the water round to warm the pot and then empty it away.

5. Put into the teapot one heaped teaspoonful of tea per person and one for the pot. (If you must use teabags, ignore the one for the pot.)

6. Take the kettle to the pot and fill to the required level with the freshly boiled water.

7. Allow to stand for two minutes (if you like your tea weak) or four minutes (if you like your tea strong). (Do *not* stir!)

8. Pour into cups through a strainer (preferably silver).

9. The milk, if required, goes in after the tea.

Scones

Delicious cut in half and spread with home-made strawberry jam and a knob of clotted cream.

Ingredients

225 g (8 oz) self-raising flour
1 level teaspoon baking powder
40 g (1 ½ oz) softened butter
25 g (1 oz) caster sugar
1 egg
about 150 ml (¼ pint) milk

Method

Makes 8–10 scones

Lightly grease a baking sheet. Place the flour and baking powder into a bowl. Rub in the butter until the mixture looks like breadcrumbs. Stir in the sugar. Break the egg into a small bowl and whisk lightly with a fork. Add the milk. Stir this mixture into the flour and then work it into a soft dough. Try not to handle the mixture too much. It should remain a little sticky.

Turn the mixture on to a lightly floured worktop and knead gently. Roll out the mixture until it is 2 cm (¾ in.) thick. Cut into rounds with a 5-cm (2-in.) fluted pastry-cutter. Arrange on the greased baking sheet. Brush with a little milk and bake in the oven at 200°C (400°F) for about 10 minutes, until risen and golden brown.

Cut in half and eat while still warm, spread with butter or jam and cream.

If you want to eat well in England, eat three breakfasts.

W. Somerset Maugham (1874–1965)

Chickens

THERE IS NOTHING HALF SO satisfying as collecting fresh eggs for breakfast. A small patch of ground – shaded by an apple tree and put down to grass – can keep a small flock going quite happily. Buy a small chicken house to keep them warm and dry. You will need to provide them with fresh water in a drinker, and you can feed them on layers' pellets or corn, and they'll enjoy the grass as well. They'll supply you with eggs from January to September or October (longer if you give them supplementary lighting), and they are great at controlling slugs. Just don't let them loose in the garden – they'll wreak havoc, even the tiny bantams.

Half a dozen hens in lay will be plenty for a family of four, but as they get older they go off lay completely, and unless you want to give them the chop (I never have the heart – Harriet the light Sussex has just fallen off her perch at twelve years old), you'll need to add to your flock.

Foxes will take them now and then unless you have a completely enclosed run or (as we have) an electric wire running along the top of the enclosure.

English Fare
English Fare

Best Layers

light Sussex (white with a black-and-white hackle and black tail)
  – 150–200 eggs a year
marans (cuckoo-type mottling in light and dark grey) – 150 eggs
  a year*
buff Orpingtons (orange buff with lots of feathers, almost spher-
  ical – inclined to go broody) – 160 eggs a year
ancona (green-tinged black-and-white feathers) – 160 eggs a year
Welsummer (orange-brown body and black tail) – 150 eggs a
  year*
Rhode Island red (orange-brown feathers) – 190 eggs a year.

* The darkest brown eggs.

Fish Pie

Perfect with a glass of chilled white wine!

Ingredients

For the topping:
1 kg (2 lb) potatoes
150 ml (¼ pint) milk
knob of butter

For the filling:
400 g (14 oz) white fish – e.g. cod
200 g (7 oz) smoked haddock
100 g (3 ½ oz) peeled prawns
600 ml (1 pint) milk
50 g (2 oz) butter
50 g (2 oz) plain flour
salt and freshly ground pepper
2 tablespoons freshly chopped chives
2 eggs, hard-boiled and halved
50 g (2 oz) Cheddar cheese

Method *Serves 4–6*

Boil and mash the potatoes. Add the 150 ml (¼ pint) of milk and the knob of butter. Put the white fish and smoked fish in a saucepan with the remaining milk. Bring to the boil. Cover and remove from the heat. Leave until the fish can be flaked with a fork. Strain, keeping the milk. Skin the fish, removing any bones, and divide into chunks. Heat the rest of the butter in a pan, stir in the flour and cook for a minute. Gradually blend in the milk from the fish and slowly bring to the boil, stirring until thickened. Add the seasoning and the chives.

Lightly grease a 1 ½-litre (2 ½-pint) oven-proof dish. A large, shallow one is best. Evenly distribute the chunks of fish, prawns and egg in the dish, then pour the white sauce over the mixture. Cover with the mashed potato and fluff up the surface with a fork. Grate a little Cheddar cheese over the top. Put in the oven at 190°C (375°F) for about 30 minutes until golden brown.

Sir,

The hymn 'Onward, Christian Soldiers' sung to the right tune and in a not-too-brisk tempo makes a very good egg-timer. If you put the egg into boiling water and sing all five verses and chorus, the egg will be just right when you come to 'Amen'.

Letter in the *Daily Telegraph* (1983)

Traditional Steak and Kidney Pudding

Ingredients

For the suet pastry:

220 g (½ lb) plain flour
110 g (¼ lb) beef suet
¼ teaspoon salt
½ teaspoon baking powder
cold water

For the filling:

450 g (1 lb) quality beef steak, chopped
110 g (¼ lb) ox kidney, chopped
1 medium onion, chopped
2 tablespoons plain flour
salt and pepper
150 ml (¼ pint) water

Method
Serves 4–6

Put all the dry ingredients for the pastry together and add the water gradually to make a soft dough. Gently knead it together. Use two-thirds of the pastry to carefully line a 1 kg (2 lb) pudding basin, saving the other third for the lid. Make sure some of the pudding-basin pastry overlaps for a good seal with the lid.

Put the beef, kidney and onion in a bowl and toss well in the seasoned flour. Pack the mixture into the lined basin and top up with water, just covering the meat. Put the lid on and seal carefully. Cover with buttered greaseproof paper, with a pleat to allow for rising. Tie the paper round the basin with string. Steam in a double saucepan for about 6 hours. (That's why you don't often see it on a menu!)

Bring to the table in the basin with a linen napkin tied round the rim. Have a jug of boiling water ready to top up the gravy if necessary. This is what we call a proper steak and kidney pudding!

Spotted Dick

Ingredients

100 g (3½ oz) self-raising flour
a pinch of salt
75 g (2½ oz) shredded suet
75 g (2½ oz) fresh breadcrumbs
50 g (2 oz) caster sugar
170 g (6 oz) currants
grated rind of one lemon
5 tablespoons milk

Method   *Serves 4–6*

Take a large mixing bowl and place in it all the dry ingredients. Mix thoroughly. Make a hollow in the centre and gradually add the milk, mixing it in to make a soft dough. Knead gently until the dough is smooth. Flour the worktop and then tip the mixture out on to it. Roll it out into an oblong about 23 cm × 30 cm (9 in. × 12 in.).

Next, bring a large pan of water to the boil. Take one large sheet of greaseproof paper and make a pleat in the centre. Wrap the pudding in the paper, to make a Christmas-cracker shape. Tie each end with string. Steam or boil for 2 hours. Serve with hot custard.

Apple Pie

Ingredients

750 g (1 ½ lb) cooking apples, peeled, cored and sliced thinly
75 g (3 oz) soft brown sugar
½ teaspoon ground cinnamon
½ teaspoon grated nutmeg
4 cloves
170 g (6 oz) shortcrust pastry

Method
Serves 4–6 people

Layer the apples with the sugar and spices in a 850-ml (1 ½ -pint) pie dish. Roll out the pastry so that it is 5 cm (2 in.) larger than the pie dish. Cut off the outer circle of the pastry and lay it on the rim of the pie dish. Brush it with water. Lift the pastry on to the rolling pin and place it over the apples, making sure that the edges are sealed. Trim away the excess pastry with a knife and indent the rim with your thumb, all the way round. Slip the knife into the centre of the pie to make a hole. Brush the pastry with water, sprinkle on a little sugar and bake in a preheated oven at 200°C (400°F) for 30 to 40 minutes.

Serve hot or cold with clotted cream.

The Queen of Hearts she made some tarts,
    All on a summer's day;
The Knave of Hearts he stole those tarts,
    And took them quite away.

The Queen of Hearts had made those tarts
    To feast a chosen few;
And on the shelf put them herself,
    Saying, 'They'll surely do.'
For she'd sent out her cards about
    To every King and Queen,
Who in the pack, in red and black,
    Are always to be seen.

Each noble pair in state came there,
    The royal board was spread;
The King with verve began to serve,
    The Queen she cut the bread.
The soup and fish, and many a dish,
    They ate with laughter gay,
And now the plum-pudding was come,
    As though 'twere Christmas Day.

The Queen called then her serving men,
    Unconscious of disaster;
'Remove,' said she, 'this dish from me,
    And put it to your master.'
All wondered what else she had got,
    When to their joy she bade
The Knave of Hearts to bring the tarts
    Which she herself had made.

The Knave he went as he'd been sent,
    But soon returned to say,
'Some malcontent on thieving bent
    Has stole the tarts away.'
Oh, then each guest did try his best
    A cheerful look to wear,
As if to say, 'Don't mind it, pray,
    We really do not care.'

Then spoke the Knave in accents grave,
    'Your Majesty,' said he,
'I think I know who is the foe –
    Your tom cat it must be;
He looked at me quite guiltily,
    And ran away full speed,
Which surely shows he full well knows
    'Twas he who did the deed.'

English Fare

Then from his seat in anger great,
    Up rose the King of Hearts:
'Oh, Knave, for shame!' he did exclaim,
    'Do cats eat damson tarts?
It's my belief thou art the thief,
    But that I soon will see;
So go and call my servants all,
    And bid them come to me.'

Up bustled then the serving men,
    Up bustled all the maids;
And there they stand a goodly band,
    According to their grades.
The Knave, 'tis said, was at their head,
    For he was reckoned chief:
'Now by this ring,' exclaimed the King,
    'I'll soon find out the thief.'

The maidens then, and serving men,
    Stared at the King of Hearts:
'I see,' said he, right solemnly,
    'Who stole the damson tarts:
His lips retain the purple stain
    Of juice upon them yet;
To hide his sin, his mouth and chin
    To wipe, he did forget.'

All looked to see who it could be,
   Except the Knave, I wot,
Who did begin to wipe his chin,
   Though it no stain had got.
Oh, then up starts the King of Hearts,
   'Deceitful Knave!' cried he,
'Now straight confess your wickedness,
   Upon your bended knee.'

Up rose the Queen with bitter mien,
   'Oh, sire!' she cried, 'did I
Prepare a treat for Knaves to eat?
   He surely ought to die.'
The King looked grave at Queen and Knave,
   Quoth he, 'The tarts are eaten;
But mercy still shall be my will,
   So let the thief be beaten.'

Anonymous (1782)

Beef

The meat that Britain was built on. There are, at present, 10.5 million head of cattle in Britain; 2.1 million of them are used in dairy breeding, and 1.8 million in beef breeding. Progeny from the national dairy herd that are not required for dairy replacement purposes can be used for beef – 50 per cent of the cattle used for beef in Britain are unwanted dairy beasts.

There are many native British breeds of beef cattle, named by their region. Of the English ones, these are among the best:

Hereford
South Devon
red poll
red Devon
Lincolnshire red
beef shorthorn

If you really don't mind going north of the border for your beef, then you can settle for Aberdeen Angus or belted Galloway. And then there is the Welsh black. Ah, but a red poll ...

Beef cattle may be male or female, but the males grow faster than the females. Heffers are at least two years old before they can calve, and they then tend to be put in calf once a year – either by natural means or by artificial insemination (AI). The gestation period is 285 days (9 months). Beef calves are withdrawn from their natural mother in a dairy herd after two to three days and are then either adopted by another 'multiple suckler' cow or a drinking dispenser – or a bucket!

They can take solids at twelve weeks. Cows graze in summer and are fed with hay or silage in winter along with concentrates. Cereal-based diets are also used to produce a faster 'finished' animal. Beef cattle are slaughtered at between twelve and twenty-six months, depending on their feeding regime and development.

Yorkshire Puddings

To serve with roast beef. They should look as if they have been blown up with a bicycle pump!

Ingredients

100 g (3 ½ oz) plain flour
a pinch of salt
1 egg
300 ml (½ pint) milk
a little lard or dripping

Method   *Makes 8 small puddings*

Sift the flour and salt into a basin. Make a hollow in the centre and crack in the egg. Use a wooden spoon to beat the egg and gradually mix in the flour. Add the milk very slowly, beating the batter well until it is smooth and creamy. Place a little knob of the lard or dripping into the base of 8 bun tins or trays and place in a very hot oven – around 220°C (430°F) until the fat is melted and beginning to shimmer. Take the tray out of the oven and pour in the batter to the rim of each bun tin. Return to the oven as quickly as possible and cook for 25 to 30 minutes until risen and golden brown.

Serve as a starter with gravy, and then again with the roast beef.

Food and Drink No English Home Should Be Without

fruit cake

digestive biscuits

Mr Kipling's Almond Slices

Earl Grey and lapsang tea

Marmite

Colman's English mustard

Weetabix

Branston Pickle

Lincolnshire pork sausages

Battenberg cake

freshly laid eggs

Pimm's No. 1 cup

Duchy biscuits

custard creams

claret

bourbons

pickled onions

fresh parsley

Oxo cubes

English Fare

Heinz tomato ketchup
Hovis
Harvey's Bristol Cream
lardy cake
butter
dry-cured back bacon
builders' tea
baked beans
Cox's apples
Arctic roll
tinned pears
jelly
Bird's custard

tomato soup
Lyle's golden syrup
malt vinegar
sea salt
Taylor's Vintage Port
Kendal mint cake
HP Sauce
Wensleydale cheese
Bourneville chocolate

England, Our England

Jersey royals
Little Gem lettuce
Baxter's royal game soup
frozen peas
teacakes
horseradish sauce
Bisto
porridge

kippers
local honey
home-made jam
mint sauce
damson gin (better than sloe)
Jacob's Cream Crackers
nutmeg
Frank Cooper's Oxford marmalade
sardines
Worcester sauce
oat cakes
roast beef
chocolate-coated orange peel

The Englishman Abroad

WE DO NOT HAVE A PARTICULARLY good reputation for carrying ourselves well overseas. I am not talking about extremes of behaviour – the worst excesses of football hooliganism and hen parties from eastern counties. No. Even the most respectable Englishman does not always find the best in himself when he crosses the Channel.

P. G. Wodehouse encapsulates that feeling we know so well:

Into the face of the young man who sat on the terrace of the Hôtel Magnifique in Cannes there had crept a look of furtive shame, the shifty, hangdog look which announces that an Englishman is about to talk French.

The Luck of the Bodkins (1935),
P. G. Wodehouse (1881–1975)

Pray tell me the time,
It is six,
It is seven,
It's half past eleven,
It's twenty to two,
I want thirteen stamps,
Does your child have convulsions?
Please bring me some rhubarb,
I need a shampoo,
How much is that hat?
I desire some red stockings,
My mother is married,
These boots are too small,
My aunt has a cold,
Shall we go to the opera?
This meat is disgusting,
Is this the town hall?

My cousin is deaf,
Kindly bring me a hatchet,
Pray pass me the pepper,
What pretty cretonne,

The Englishman Abroad

What time is the train?
It is late,
It is early,
It's running on schedule,
It's here,
It has gone,
I've written six letters,
I've written no letters,
Pray fetch me a horse,
I have need of a groom,
This isn't my passport,
This isn't my hatbox,
please show me the way
To Napoleon's tomb.

The weather is cooler,
The weather is hotter,
Prey fasten my corsets,
Please bring me my cloak,
I've lost my umbrella,
I'm in a great hurry,
I'm going,
I'm staying,
D'you mind if I smoke?
This mutton is tough,
There's a mouse in my bedroom,

This egg is delicious,
This soup is too thick,
Please bring me a trout,
What an excellent pudding,
Pray hand me my gloves,
I'm going to be sick!

'Useless Useful Phrases' (1961),
Noël Coward (1899–1973)

I take it you already know
Of tough and bough and cough and dough?
Others may stumble, but not you
On hiccough, thorough, laugh and through?
Well done! And now you wish perhaps
To learn of these familiar traps?

Beware of heard, a dreadful word,
That looks like beard and sounds like bird,
And dead: it's said like bed, not bead,
For goodness' sake, don't call it deed!
Watch out for meat and great and threat,
They rhyme with suite and straight and debt.

A moth is not a moth in mother,
Nor both in bother, broth in brother,
And here is not a match for there,
Nor dear and fear for bear and pear,
And then there's does and rose and lose –
Just look them up: and goose and choose
And cork and front and word and ward,
And font and front and word and sword,

And do and go and thwart and cart –
Come, come, I've hardly made a start!

A dreadful language? Man alive,
I'd mastered it when I was five!

'Hints on Pronunciation for Foreigners' (1965),
T.S.W.

It is good to be on your guard against an Englishman who speaks French perfectly; he is very likely to be a card-sharper or an attaché in the diplomatic service.

W. Somerset Maugham (1874–1965)

Parlez-vous franglais?

C'est un doddle.

Si vous êtes un fluent English-speaker, et si vous avez un 'O' level français, franglais est un morceau de gâteau.

Un 'O' level de French est normalement inutile. Un nothing. Un wash-out. Les habitants de la France ne parlent pas 'O' level French. Ils ne comprennent pas 'O' level French. Un 'O' level en français est un passeport à nowhere.

Let's Parler Franglais (1979),
Miles Kington (1941–)

Or, as a friend of mine once put it, '*Étouffe cela pour une alouette.*' (Which roughly translated means 'Stuff that for a lark.')

OUR DRESS WILL OFTEN GIVE us away when we are abroad, and we can't for the life of us understand why. What is it about the baggy shorts that come down to mid-calf level, the large white trainers with black socks and the bright-red Manchester United football shirt that tells the other Europeans we are English? After all, there are Manchester United supporters all over the world.

Whatever happened to the days when gentlemen travelling abroad would wear a Lock and Co. Panama hat, a cream linen suit from Gieves and Hawkes and a pair of bespoke shoes from Lobb? The shirt would be a white cotton batiste from Turnbull and Asser, and the diagonally striped silk tie would be tied in a full Windsor. Here's how:

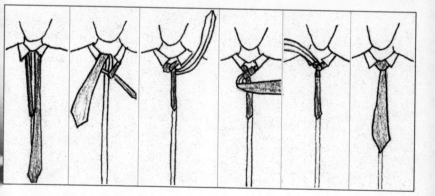

The world still consists of two clearly divided groups: the English and the foreigners. One group consists of less than 50 million people; the other of 3,950 million. The latter group does not really count.

How to Be Decadent (1977),
George Mikes (1912–1987)

In tropical climes there are certain times of day
When all the citizens retire
To tear their clothes off and perspire.
It's one of those rules that the greatest fools obey,
Because the sun is much too sultry
And one must avoid its ultry-violet ray.
 Papalaka papalaka papalaka boo,
 Papalaka papalaka papalaka boo!
 Digariga digariga digariga doo,
 Digariga digariga digariga doo!
The natives grieve when the white men leave their huts,
Because they're obviously, definitely nuts!

Mad dogs and Englishmen
Go out in the midday sun.
The Japanese don't care to,
The Chinese wouldn't dare to,
Hindoos and Argentines sleep firmly from twelve to one,
But Englishmen detest a siesta.
In the Philippines
There are lovely screens
To protect you from the glare.

England, Our England

In the Malay states
There are hats like plates
Which the Britishers won't wear.
At twelve noon
The natives swoon
And no further work is done,
But mad dogs and Englishmen
Go out in the midday sun.

It's such a surprise for the Eastern eyes to see
That though the English are effete,
They're quite impervious to heat,
When the white man rides, every native hides in glee,
Because the simple creatures hope he
Will impale his solar topee on a tree.
   Bolyboly, bolyboly, bolyboly baa,
   Bolyboly, bolyboly, bolyboly baa!
   Habaninny, habaninny, habaninny haa,
   Habaninny, habaninny, habaninny haa!

Mad dogs and Englishmen
Go out in the midday sun.
The toughest Burmese bandit
Can never understand it,
In Rangoon the heat of noon is just what the natives shun,
They put their Scotch or rye down and lie down.

In a jungle town where the sun beats down to the rage of man
or beast,
The English garb of the English sahib merely gets a bit more
creased,
In Bangkok
At twelve o'clock
They foam at the mouth and run,
But mad dogs and Englighmen
Go out in the midday sun.

Mad dogs and Englighmen
Go out in the midday sun.
The smallest Malay rabbit
Deplores this foolish habit,
In Hong Kong they strike a gong and fire off a noon-day gun
To reprimand each inmate who's in late.
In the mangrove swamps where the python romps there is
peace from twelve till two,
Even caribous lie around and snooze for there's nothing else
to do.
In Bengal
To move at all
Is seldom if ever done,
But mad dogs and Englishmen go out in the midday sun.

'Mad Dogs and Englishmen' (1931),
Noël Coward (1899–1973)

*I don't hold with abroad, and I think that foreigners
speak English when our backs are turned.*

The Naked Civil Servant (1968),
Quentin Crisp (1908–99)

Words and Music

Only ever read one book: White Fang. So good, never felt the need to read another.

Attributed to Nancy Mitford's father,
Lord Redesdale (1878–1958)

Charles Dickens
(1812–70)

A N ENGLISH AUTHOR WHOSE tales of everyday Victorian
life are vividly evocative of an age of class-ridden society, privilege and poverty, pride before a fall, hunger, waste,
profligacy, wit, cruelty, wickedness and, occasionally, good
nature. Their imagery is rich in the extreme, and the original
engravings – many of them by Hablot K. Browne (who took
the name of 'Phiz') – are superb works of art. Many of Dickens's novels were first published in serial form in magazines.
Dickens married Catherine Hogarth (daughter of the editor of
the *Evening Chronicle*) in 1836 and they had ten children. He
left her for the actress Ellen Ternan in 1858. He died in 1870
at his home, Gad's Hill, near Rochester in Kent, and is buried
in Poets' Corner in Westminster Abbey.

The Novels

The Pickwick Papers (1836–37)
Oliver Twist – 1837–39
Nicholas Nickleby – 1838–39
The Old Curiosity Shop – 1840–41
Barnaby Rudge – 1841
A Christmas Carol – 1843
Martin Chuzzlewit – 1843–44
The Chimes – 1844
The Cricket on the Hearth – 1845
The Battle of Life – 1846
Pictures From Italy – 1846
Dombey and Son – 1846–48
The Haunted Man and the Ghost's Bargain – 1848
David Copperfield – 1849–50
Bleak House – 1852–53
Hard Times – 1854
Little Dorrit – 1855–57
A Tale of Two Cities – 1859
Great Expectations – 1860–61
Our Mutual Friend – 1864–65
No Thoroughfare – 1867
The Mystery of Edwin Drood (unfinished) – 1870
The Lazy Tour of Two Idle Apprentices – pub. 1890

The Brontë Sisters

THE BRONTË SISTERS (five of them) were the daughters of Patrick Brontë, an Irishman and the curate of Haworth in Yorkshire. Their mother died in 1821, leaving Branwell (the brother), Charlotte, Emily, Anne and their two elder sisters in the care of their aunt, Elizabeth Branwell. The two elder sisters died while away at the Clergy Daughters' School in Cowan Bridge in 1825 (the school was used as the model for Lowood in *Jane Eyre*) and the remaining children returned to continue their education at home, where they created an imaginary world and where their writing began.

Branwell, who had a liking for the bottle, died in 1848. The sisters wrote, at first, under the pseudonyms of Currer (Charlotte), Ellis (Emily) and Acton (Anne) Bell, finally revealing their true identities when speculation suggested that the three names applied to only one author.

The Novels

CHARLOTTE BRONTË (1816–55)

The Professor (unpublished in her lifetime)
Jane Eyre – 1847
Shirley – 1849
Villette – 1853

EMILY JANE BRONTË (1818–48)

Wuthering Heights – 1847

ANNE BRONTË (1820–49)

Agnes Grey – 1847
The Tenant of Wildfell Hall – 1848

Reader, I married him. A quiet wedding we had: he and I, the parson and the clerk, were alone present. When we got back from church, I went into the kitchen of the manor-house, where Mary was cooking the dinner, and John cleaning the knives, and I said:–

'Mary, I have been married to Mr Rochester this morning.' The housekeeper and her husband were both of that decent phlegmatic order of people, to whom one may at any time safely communicate a remarkable piece of news without incurring the danger of having one's ears pierced by some shrill ejaculation, and subsequently stunned by a torrent of wordy wonderment. Mary did look up, and she did stare at me; the ladle with which she was basting a pair of chickens roasting at the fire, did for some three minutes hang suspended in air; and for the same space of time John's knives also had rest from the polishing process: but Mary, bending again over the roast, said only:–

'Have you, Miss? Well, for sure!'

Jane Eyre (1847),
Charlotte Brontë (1816–55)

Poet Laureate

APPOINTED FOR LIFE since John Dryden in the time of Charles II, by letters patent, the poet laureate has no official duties but is expected to come up with works to mark important royal occasions. The annual stipend from the civil list is minimal and some form of alcohol usually forms a part of it (in Dryden's time 'a butt of Canary wine'). When the poet laureate dies, the names of possible successors are proposed by the prime minister for the sovereign's approval.

Gulielmus Peregrinus – appointed by Richard the Lionheart
Master Henry – appointed by Henry III
Geoffrey Chaucer – c.1343–1400
John Kay – appointed by Edward IV
Bernard André of Toulouse – appointed by Henry VII
John Skelton – appointed by Henry VIII
Edmund Spenser – died in 1599
Samuel Daniel – 1599
Ben Jonson – 1619
Sir William Davenant – 1637
John Dryden – 1670

Nahum Tate – 1692
Nicholas Rowe – 1715
Reverend Laurence Eusden – 1718
Colley Cibber – 1730
William Whitehead – 1757
Rev. Thomas Warton (William Mason declined) – 1785
Henry James Pye – 1790
Robert Southey (Sir Walter Scott declined) – 1813
William Wordsworth – 1843
Alfred, Lord Tennyson (Samuel Russell declined) – 1850
Alfred Austin (William Morris declined) – 1896
Robert Bridges – 1913
John Masefield – 1930
Cecil Day-Lewis – 1967
Sir John Betjeman – 1972
Ted Hughes (Philip Larkin declined) – 1984
Andrew Motion – 1999

William Shakespeare
(1564–1616)

ENGLAND'S GREATEST DRAMATIST, who was probably born (and certainly died) on St George's Day – 23 April – at Stratford-upon-Avon.

The Complete Works

Titus Andronicus – 1590

Richard III – 1591

King John – 1591–98

Henry VI, Part 1 – 1592

Henry VI, Part 2 – 1592

Henry VI, Part 3 – 1592

The Taming of the Shrew – 1592

The Two Gentlemen of Verona – 1592–93

The Comedy of Errors – 1592–94

Venus and Adonis – 1593

The Rape of Lucrece – 1594

Love's Labour's Lost – 1595

Romeo and Juliet – 1595

Richard II – 1595
A Midsummer Night's Dream – 1595–96
The Merchant of Venice – 1596–98
The Merry Wives of Windsor – 1597
Henry IV, Part 1 – 1597
Henry IV, Part 2 – 1597
Much Ado About Nothing – 1598–99
Julius Caesar – 1599
The Passionate Pilgrim – 1599
As You Like It – 1599
Henry V – 1599
Twelfth Night – 1601
Hamlet – 1601
The Phoenix and the Turtle – 1601
Troilus and Cressida – 1602
Othello – 1602–04
All's Well That Ends Well – 1603–04
Measure for Measure – 1604
King Lear – 1605–06
Macbeth – 1606
Antony and Cleopatra – 1606–07
Pericles – 1606–08
Timon of Athens – c.1607
Coriolanus – 1608
A Lover's Complaint – 1609
Sonnets – 1609

Words and Music

Cymbeline – 1609–10
The Winter's Tale – 1610–11
The Tempest – 1611
Henry VIII – 1613
The Two Noble Kinsmen – 1634

Jane Austen
(1775–1817)

HAROLD MACMILLAN SUGGESTED that one of Margaret Thatcher's problems was that she did not read enough Jane Austen. Read them all. Then read them again.

Born and brought up by her clergyman father in Steventon, Hampshire, she lived for a time, unhappily, in Bath (1801–06), in Southampton (1806–09) and latterly in Chawton, Hampshire (1809–17). She is buried in Winchester Cathedral.

The Novels

Lady Susan (novella) – 1805
The Watsons (incomplete novel) – 1805
Sense and Sensibility – 1811
Pride and Prejudice – 1813
Mansfield Park – 1814
Emma – 1816
Sanditon (incomplete novel) – 1817
Persuasion – 1817
Northanger Abbey – 1817 (written in 1798)

Justifiably one of the most popular English writers, Jane Austen's work offers sublime escape into the world of Regency England and is wonderfully readable. Asked to quote her, most would come up with the opening sentence to *Pride and Prejudice*:

> It is a truth universally acknowledged, that a single man in possession of a good fortune must be in want of a wife.

The opening sentence to *Emma* is every bit as engaging:

> Emma Woodhouse, handsome, clever, and rich, with a comfortable home and happy disposition, seemed to unite some of the best blessings of existence; and had lived nearly twenty-one years in the world with very little to distress or vex her.

Both introductions give a hint of the waspishness that is to follow – one of Austen's greatest charms – a quality that is often missing in film and television adaptations, when the narrator's voice on the page is replaced by on-screen action. Her novels might have been written in the early nineteenth century, but thanks to her acute observation of personality traits and the high value she places on common sense, her writings are as valid today as they were nearly two hundred years ago.

This is one of my favourite passages from *Emma*:

Mrs Goddard was the mistress of a school – not of a seminary, or an establishment, or any thing which professed, in long sentences of refined nonsense, to combine liberal acquirements with elegant morality, upon new principles and new systems – and where young ladies for enormous pay might be screwed out of health and into vanity – but a real, honest, old-fashioned boarding-school, where a reasonable quantity of accomplishments were sold at a reasonable price, and where girls might be sent to be out of the way and scramble themselves into a little education, without any danger of coming back prodigies.

Best-Selling English Books

Single Volumes

The Bible
The Book of Common Prayer, Thomas Cranmer
The Pilgrim's Progress, John Bunyan
The Book of Martyrs, John Foxe
Harry Potter and the Philosopher's Stone, J. K. Rowling
And Then There Were None, Agatha Christie
The Lord of the Rings, J. R. R. Tolkien
Harry Potter and the Half-Blood Prince, J. K. Rowling
Harry Potter and the Chamber of Secrets, J. K. Rowling
Harry Potter and the Order of the Phoenix, J. K. Rowling
Harry Potter and the Prisoner of Azkaban, J. K. Rowling
Harry Potter and the Goblet of Fire, J. K. Rowling
Watership Down, Richard Adams
The Tale of Peter Rabbit, Beatrix Potter

Series

Harry Potter, J. K. Rowling
Noddy, Enid Blyton

England, Our England

Peter Rabbit, Beatrix Potter
Clifford the Big Red Dog, Norman Bridwell
Mr Men, Roger Hargreaves
Guinness Book of Records
The Chronicles of Narnia, C. S. Lewis
Thomas the Tank Engine, Rev. W. V. Awdry
Winnie the Pooh, A. A. Milne

Words and Music

The English may not like music, but they absolutely love the noise it makes.

Sir Thomas Beecham

England's Best Composers
(and Some of Their Best Bits)

JOHN TAVERNER (*c.*1490–1545)

Magnificat à 4
Missa 'Gloria tibi Trinitas'

THOMAS TALLIS (*c.*1505–85)

Spem in alium
If ye love me

WILLIAM BYRD (*c.*1543–1623)

Ave verum corpus
Great Service

HENRY PURCELL (*c.*1659–95)

Dido and Aeneas
The Faery Queen

JEREMIAH CLARKE (*c.*1674–1707)

'Trumpet Voluntary'

Words and Music

GEORGE FRIDERIC HANDEL (1685–1759)*

The Messiah
Water Music
Music for the Royal Fireworks

SIR ARTHUR SULLIVAN (1842–1900)

HMS Pinafore
The Pirates of Penzance
The Mikado

SIR EDWARD ELGAR (1857–1934)

The Dream of Gerontius
Cello Concerto
Enigma Variations
Pomp and Circumstance Marches

SIR HUBERT PARRY (1848–1918)

Jerusalem
I Was Glad

FREDERICK DELIUS (1862–1934)

In a Summer Garden
The Walk to the Paradise Garden
On Hearing the First Cuckoo in Spring

* He was born in Germany, but spent most of his life in England

England, Our England

RALPH VAUGHAN WILLIAMS (1872–1958)

The Lark Ascending
Fantasia on a Theme by Thomas Tallis

GUSTAV HOLST (1874–1934)

The Planets
The Hymn of Jesus

JOHN IRELAND (1879–1962)

Sonatina
A London Overture
Piano Concerto in E Flat Major

SIR ARNOLD BAX (1883–1953)

Tintagel
This World's Joie
Symphony No. 6

GEORGE BUTTERWORTH (1885–1916)

A Shropshire Lad
The Banks of Green Willow

SIR ARTHUR BLISS (1891–1975)

A Colour Symphony
Things to Come

Word and Music

Sir William Walton (1902–83)

Façade
Spitfire Prelude
Belshazzar's Feast
Henry V

Sir Michael Tippett (1905–98)

A Child of Our Time
The Midsummer Marriage
King Priam

Sir Benjamin Britten (1913–76)

Serenade for Tenor, Horn and Strings
The Young Person's Guide to the Orchestra
Peter Grimes
Billy Budd
The Turn of the Screw
War Requiem

Sir Peter Maxwell Davies (1934–)

Eight Songs for a Mad King
Return to Stromness
Taverner

England, Our England

SIR HARRISON BIRTWISTLE (1934–)

Gawain's Journey
The Mask of Orpheus

SIR JOHN TAVENER (1944–)

The Whale
Akhmatova: Rekviem
The Protecting Veil

MARK-ANTHONY TURNAGE (1960–)

The Silver Tassie
Blood on the Floor

The Gilbert and Sullivan Operas

BELOVED OF MANY AND DESPISED by schoolboys who have to play girls in them, the 'Savoy Operas', often known simply as 'Gee and Ess', contain some of the finest English romantic and comic songs. The words were written by William Schwenck Gilbert (1836–1911), and the music by Arthur Seymour Sullivan (1842–1900). According to the American composer and lyricist Stephen Sondheim, W. S. Gilbert still ranks as the greatest lyricist ever. The 'patter songs', such as 'I am the very model of a modern major general' (*The Pirates of Penzance*) and the Lord Chancellor's 'Nightmare Song' (from *Iolanthe*), will test the crispness of diction of any baritone.

Famously incompatible, Gilbert and Sullivan had many fallouts, and Sullivan always felt that his musical talent was wasted on such trivial productions. But then who can hum a tune from his opera *Ivanhoe*?

The 'Savoy Operas' were produced in the following order:

> *Thespis* (or *The Gods Grown Old*) – 1871
> *Trial by Jury* – 1875
> *The Sorcerer* – 1877

England, Our England

HMS Pinafore (or *The Lass That Loved a Sailor*) – 1878
The Pirates of Penzance (or *The Slave of Duty*) – 1879
Patience (or *Bunthorne's Bride*) – 1881
Iolanthe (or *The Peer and the Peri*) – 1882
Princess Ida (or *Castle Adamant*) – 1884
The Mikado (or *The Town of Titipu*) – 1885
Ruddigore (or *The Witch's Curse*) – 1887
The Yeomen of the Guard (or *The Merryman and His Maid*) – 1888
The Gondoliers (or *The King of Barataria*) – 1889
Utopia Limited (or *The Flowers of Progress*) – 1893
The Grand Duke (or *The Statutory Duel*) – 1896

'Greensleeves'

'GREENSLEEVES' IS TWICE mentioned in Shakespeare's *The Merry Wives of Windsor* and is first referred to in 1580 in the register of the Stationers' Company, where it is called 'a new Northern Dittye', but there is evidence that it dates from even earlier than this. It is sometimes suggested that the tune was written by Henry VIII, but there seems to be no proof of this.

> Alas! My love, you do me wrong
> To cast me off discourteously;
> And I have loved you so long,
> Delighting in your company.
>
> Greensleeves was all my joy!
> Greensleeves was my delight!
> Greensleeves was my heart of gold!
> And who but my Lady Greensleeves!
>
> I bought thee petticoats of the best,
> The cloth so fine as fine as might be;

I gave thee jewels for thy chest,
And all this cost I spent on thee.

Thy smock of silk, both fair and white,
With gold embroidered gorgeously;
Thy petticoat of sendal white:
And these I bought thee gladly.

Thy gown was of the grassy green,
The sleeves of satin hanging by;
Which made thee be our harvest queen:
And yet thou wouldest not love me!

Greensleeves now farewell! Adieu!
God I pray to prosper thee!
For I am still thy lover true:
Come once again and love me!

Greensleeves was all my joy!
Greensleeves was my delight!
Greensleeves was my heart of gold!
And who but my Lady Greensleeves!

'Greensleeves' (date unknown), Anon.

Masters of the King's/Queen's Music

A N HONORARY POST in the royal household. There are no
stated duties, but it is expected that the incumbent will
write music to commemorate royal events such as marriages,
anniversaries and deaths, and ceremonial occasions. The title
was created in 1626 by Charles I. The current incumbent is
appointed for ten years; previous appointments were for life.

Nicholas Lanier – 1626

Louis Grabu – 1666

Nicholas Staggins – 1674

John Eccles – 1700

Maurice Greene – 1735

William Boyce – 1755

John Stanley – 1779

William Parsons – 1786

William Shield – 1817

Christian Kramer – 1829

Franz Cramer – 1829

George Frederick Anderson – 1848

Sir William George Cusins – 1870

England, Our England

Professor Sir Walter Parratt – 1893
Sir Edward Elgar – 1924
Sir Henry Walford Davies – 1934
Sir Arnold Bax – 1942
Sir Arthur Bliss – 1953
Malcolm Williamson – 1975
Sir Peter Maxwell Davies – 2004

Play Up and
Play the Game

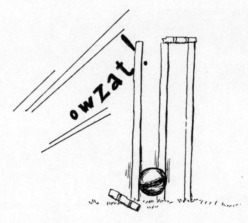

I DO NOT PLAY A LOT OF SPORT. I garden instead. And walk. Quite a lot. But I do enjoy going to Wimbledon every year and, occasionally, being invited into the royal box. It is a splendid affair. Very low key. And polite. And affable. And great fun. There is no standing on ceremony; in fact, one is instructed not to stand up if one is sitting down eating when a member of the Royal Family enters. It is usually the Duke of Kent. The Queen came in her Silver Jubilee year, in 1977, but I don't think she's been since. That may be why we haven't had a winner.

We are instructed to arrive at the royal box for about 11.30 a.m. We are given a parking permit and can leave the car just across from the entrance in a little field, which is handy. We are greeted at the large glass doors by a uniformed member of the armed forces and led past the glass cases where the trophies sit, bathed in spotlights – the cup for the men's singles and the plate for the ladies'. Very, very shiny.

We climb the stairs and are taken straight out to our seats. There is no tennis as yet, but they like to let us know exactly where we are sitting. Then the cushions on the bottle-green Lloyd Loom chairs are tilted up to show that we have arrived, and we are led back inside to the reception area and offered a glass of champagne.

At noon we sit down for lunch at round tables of eight.

Your neighbour might be a past Wimbledon champion or a member of the club (of whom there are only 375). There is a cold starter, then a choice of a fish dish or something meaty with red or white wine and water. You can have pudding or cheese. We leave the dining room and take coffee on the terrace overlooking the outside courts – a sea of well-tended greens and variously tended people. At 1 p.m., or just before, we are encouraged to take our seats for the start of play.

Princess Michael of Kent is often in the front row. Or the Duchess of Gloucester. Or both. Along with the Duke of Kent.

We watch the tennis until 3.45 p.m. It's usually terribly good. After that, we come back inside for afternoon tea – finger sandwiches, cakes, Bath buns, strawberries and cream. Then we go out again and watch the tennis – which is now even better – until rain or bad light stops play. We can usually manage to see about three matches. Unless the sun is very hot and my neck won't stay up. And then I miss bits. Then we come back in and have another glass of champagne with the committee, who are absolutely charming. Then we go home. My wife, Alison, drives. I do *love* Wimbledon.

Play Up and Play the Game

If you eliminate smoking and gambling, you will be amazed to find that almost all an Englishman's pleasures can be, and mostly are, shared by his dog.

George Bernard Shaw (1856–1950)

Cricket Explained

YOU HAVE TWO SIDES, one out in the field and one in. Each man in the side that's in goes out, and when he's out, he comes in and the next man goes in until he's out.

When they're all out, the side that's out comes in and the side that's been in goes out and tries to get those coming in out.

Sometimes you get men still in and not out. When both sides have been in and out, including not outs, that's the end of the game.

There is an alternative:

Two old men in white coats walk together to the middle of a large, green field, each carrying three long sticks and two little ones.

Each plants his three sticks in the ground 22 yards apart and puts the little sticks on top.

Then they turn round and look towards the 22 younger men at the end of the field – and it starts to rain.

Rugby

RUGBY FOOTBALL is a game I can't claim absolutely to understand in all its niceties, if you know what I mean. I can follow the broad general principles, of course. I mean to say, I know that the main scheme is to work the ball down the field somehow and deposit it over the line at the other end, and that, in order to squelch this programme, each side is allowed to put in a certain amount of assault and battery and do things to its fellow man which, if done elsewhere, would result in fourteen days without the option, coupled with some strong remarks from the bench.

And the game does funny things to people:

His air was that of a man who has been passed through a wringer, and his eyes, what you could see of them, had a strange, smouldering gleam. He was so crusted with alluvial deposits that one realised how little a mere bath would ever be able to effect. To fit him to take his place once more in polite society, he would certainly have to be sent to the cleaner's. Indeed, it was a moot point whether it wouldn't be simpler just to throw him away.

Very Good, Jeeves (1930), P. G. Wodehouse (1881–1975)

No Englishman is ever fairly beaten.

George Bernard Shaw (1856–1950)

Play Up and Play the Game

W E ENGLISH ARE DEVOTED to dogs, but we are simply in awe of horses. We like to sigh over them as they graze in green fields, with the sun rippling across their backs. We admire them when soldiers sit upon them to guard the Queen, and when mounted policemen keep order at football matches. But those who sit upon their backs and race them can take our breath away as well as our money. Clement Freud once joined their ranks – against his better judgement …

The French use the word 'ancien' not as we do to denote antiquity but to mean 'used to be'. At a recent dinner in France my host, who had done his homework with un-gallic thoroughness, introduced me as 'un ancien jockey', indicating that I have had the odd ride in public (*jockey* – like *outsider* and *walkover*, also *deadheat* – is an international word, though pronounced differently in different countries). Well, having been a jockey is one of the things for which I rather like to be remembered. It happened in my early middle-age, which is elderly for a man setting out on a career in the saddle, and was the result of a new racehorse-owner's inability to understand trainer-speak.

It was the late 1960s, Harold Wilson reigned at Number 10, and the budget for that year disallowed as an acceptable business expense all entertainment, even breakfasts, luncheon, tea and dinner bills, except where the object of hospitality was an overseas buyer. At the Newmarket sales in October I bought an Ananmestes yearling and named him Overseas Buyer. It was my intention to claim his expenses against tax: training bills would be entered as 'accommodating overseas buyer', racecourse visits as 'monitoring overseas buyer', bets as 'testing overseas buyer's market'.

I gave him to Toby Balding and some weeks after he was first saddled phoned my young trainer to ask how things were going.

Come and see him work, he said; we'll put you up.

I brought my pyjamas.

He meant ride out.

I didn't like to say that I had not ridden for thirty years, and then not seriously, unless you count the leading-rein class at the Blythburgh Gymkhana; also one journalistic day's hunting with the Quorn for the *Sunday Telegraph*, followed by five days in bed to get over it.

I was given a leg up on a three-mile hurdler due to run for his life in a seller at Newton Abbot later that week, and did what the stable lads in front of and behind and beside me did. An hour later, at breakfast, before my two-year-old was due to go out with the second lot, I asked Toby how he thought I had ridden.

Better than some bloody amateurs who try to go faster than the horse, said he. I was chuffed.

I worked for the original, pre-page-three *Sun* as a sports writer at the time. Be provocative, said the sports editor, the way sports editors do. I wrote a piece about bloody amateur jockeys going faster than their horses, and invariably putting up overweight, which could not appear in the racing papers because it is libellous to write that bets on Moonstruck are not a good idea as the owner Mr J. Johnson (7) is not only useless and unable to claim his allowance but is likely to weigh out 12lb heavy. Johnson would only have to have one leg amputated to take you to court.

Good piece, said my sports editor. Why don't you have a go?

I explained that God had not built me to race-ride, that I had not weighed under 13st 5lb since I left the army after the war, twenty years earlier.

The sports editor was unimpressed. The most unlikely people ride, he said, and I thought about it for a while, discussed becoming a latter-day Gordon Richards with Toby Balding, who was by then a friend as well as my trainer, and embarked on the campaign of losing two stone in ten weeks, in the course of which I would also achieve uncommon fitness, a shape that needed a new wardrobe and gave me near-terminal halitosis.

Reluctant to manifest my prowess in the saddle before my own countrymen, I wrote to the Irish Jockey Club for an amateur's licence, sending with my application a coolish

337

assessment of my skills on horseback signed by G. B. Balding. The Stewards of the Irish Jockey Club, in their wisdom, decided to inspect me in person, so I flew to Dublin and presented myself at their offices in Merrion Square wearing a suit with a 32-inch waist, in from 38 inches.

They looked at me with mild curiosity and the senior man asked how long I had been riding, casually, as one horsey man to another.

I can tell you that exactly, I said. It is now 4 September. I started on 29 July.

There was an intake of breaths and a splutter.

The Senior Steward looked me up and down incredulously and said: 'Have you done any speed work?'

I explained that it had been nearly all speed work; to date I had found it hard to stop horses from doing speed work ... which was surely what racing was about. Before them, I intimated, stood a man who would never be called before the men with hats for pulling a horse.

I got my licence ('What harm can he do?' said one of the Stewards) and after a warning against importuning people for mounts, I returned to England and a lesson from Mr James Lindley, a stylist whom I much admired. He watched me on the Weyhill gallops and opined that if I looked less like a ....ing policeman I might well manage to look more like a jockey. As a consequence I raised my irons and learnt to bend my spine; and in God's good time one of Toby's owners, a brave Irishman called Joe Hehir who was a power in the used tyre trade in Kilkenny and a fierce consumer of proof spirit, offered me a mount in a bumper at Naas, set to carry 12st 7lb. I could make that. There was a 7lb allowance for having ridden less than a certain number of winners. I found that difficult.

I also found it difficult to get into the jockeys' changing room. A man stopped me, said This is the jockeys' changing room.

I said I know that.

He said Well you can't go in, I mean I know who you are, but I can't let you through.

I said I am a jockey.

He said Never.

He probably had a point ... though I was in the lead first time round and realized, which I had not thought about in all the years in which I had gone racing, that you don't have to look round to see where the rest of the field is as you can hear the commentary.

Over the next eighteen months I rode when I could. Had a tricky time at Leicester when my mount squeezed me against the side of the stall and I emerged with my left foot along its spine; it took me a furlong to get back into position and I read in the following day's *Sporting Life* that I had 'dwelt at the start'. At Bath, before another race for which I had fasted and used diuretics to make the weight, my trainer looked at me in the parade ring and gave me a spoonful of salt in a glass of water to stop me from seizing up. I vomited for a mile and a half and tried to clean the saddle with my whip …

But my finest hour came in a Match race against Hugh Fraser at Haydock. I had challenged him. We both took it v. seriously, both broke ribs and sustained bruises about the body getting fit, both backed ourselves extravagantly with the on-course bookmakers – one of whom offered 5–1 on either rider to finish alone, which gave me some confidence. I had flown over the course and ridden it and walked it on the morning of the race. I was on Winter Fair, whom I had bought out of Ian Balding's yard where he was galloping companion to Mill Reef, and just a little of that brilliance rubbed off. Sir Hugh was riding one of his horses set to carry a stone less than mine and the tapes went up and because we were both pretty average jockeys and my horse was better than his, I won. Had not realized that racing was as simple as that.

I considered riding another nineteen winners to reduce my allowance but didn't think I could shed any more weight. Not long after that I hung up my 12oz saddle and my breath improved.

First Learn the Language by Clement Freud
(Stanley Paul & Co., 1992)

Play Up and Play the Game

U NDENIABLY OUR GREATEST contribution to the world of sport is football, but I have to confess it was never the game for me. This passage from *A Kestrel for a Knave* by Barry Hines brings back some uncomfortable memories of my own …

He walked into the changing room as clean and shining as a boy down for breakfast on his seaside holidays. The other boys were packed into the aisles between the rows of pegs, their hanging clothes partitioning the room into corridors. Mr Sugden was passing slowly across one end of the room, looking down the corridors and counting the boys as they changed. He was wearing a violet tracksuit. The top was embellished with cloth badges depicting numerous crests and qualifications, and on the breast a white athlete carried the Olympic torch. The legs were tucked into new white football socks, neatly folded at his ankles, and his football boots were polished as black and shiny as the bombs used by assassins in comic strips. The laces binding them had been scrubbed white, and both boots had been fastened identically: two loops of the foot and one of the ankle, and tied in a neat bow under the tab at the back.

He finished counting and rolled a football off the window sill into his hand. The leather was rich with dubbin, and the new orange lace nipped the slit as firmly as a row of surgical stitches. He tossed it up and caught it on the ends of his fingers, then turned round to Billy.

'Skyving again, Casper?'

'No, Sir, Mr Farthing wanted me; he's been talking to me.'

'I bet that was stimulating for him, wasn't it?'

'What does that mean, Sir?'

'The conversation, lad, what do you think it means?'

'No, Sir, that word, stimult … stimult-ting.'

'Stimulating, you fool, s-t-i-m-i-l-a-t-i-n-g, stimulating!'

'Yes, Sir.'

'Well get changed, lad, you're two weeks late already!'

He lifted the elastic webbing of one cuff and rotated his fist to look at his watch on the underside of his wrist.

'Some of us want a game even if you don't.'

'I've no kit, Sir.'

Mr Sugden stepped back and slowly looked Billy up and down, his top lip curling.

'Casper, you make me SICK.'

'SICK' penetrated the hubbub, which immediately decreased as the boys stopped their own conversations and turned their attention to Mr Sugden and Billy.

'Every lesson it's the same old story, "Please, Sir, I've no kit."'

The boys tittered at his whipped-dog whining impersonation.

'Every lesson for four years! And in all that time you've

342

made no attempt whatsoever to get any kit, you've skyved and scrounged and borrowed and …'

He tried this lot on one breath, and his ruddy complexion heightened and glowed like a red balloon as he held his breath and fought for another verb.

'… and … BEG …' The balloon burst and the pronunciation of the verb disintegrated.

'Why is it that everyone else can get some but you can't?'

'I don't know, Sir. My mother won't buy me any. She says it's a waste of money, especially now that I'm leaving.'

'You haven't been leaving for four years, have you?'

'No, Sir.'

'You could have bought some out of your spending money, couldn't you?'

'I don't like football, Sir.'

'What's that got to do with it?'

'I don't know, Sir. Anyway I don't get enough.'

'Get a job then. I don't …'

'I've got one, Sir.'

'Well then! You get paid, don't you?'

'Yes, Sir. But I have to gi' it to my mam. I'm still payin' her for my fines, like instalments every week.'

Mr Sugden bounced the ball on Billy's head, compressing his neck into his shoulders.

'Well you should keep out of trouble then, lad, and then …'

'I haven't been in trouble, Sir, not …'

'Shut up, lad! Shut up, before you drive me crackers!'

He hit Billy twice with the ball, holding it between both hands as though he was murdering him with a boulder. The rest of the class grinned behind each other's backs, or placed their fingers over their mouths to suppress the laughter gathering there. They watched Mr Sugden rush into his changing room, and began to giggle, stopping immediately he reappeared waving a pair of giant blue drawers.

'Here, Casper, get them on!'

He wanged them across the room, and Billy caught them flying over his head, then held them up for inspection as though he was contemplating buying. The class roared. They would have made Billy two suits and an overcoat.

'They'll not fit me, Sir.'

The class roared again and even Billy had to smile. There was only Mr Sugden not amused.

'What are you talking about, lad? You can get them on, can't you?'

'Yes, Sir.'

'Well they fit you then! Now get changed, QUICK.'

Billy found an empty peg and hung his jacket on it. He was immediately enclosed in a tight square as two lines of boys formed up, one on each side of him between the parallel curtains of clothing. He sat down on the long bench covering the shoe racks, and worked his jeans over his pumps.

Mr Sugden broke one side of the square and stood over him.

'And you want your underpants and vest off.'

'I don't wear 'em, Sir.'

As he reached up to hang his trousers on the peg, his shirt lap lifted, revealing his bare cheeks, which looked as smooth and bony as two white billiard balls. He stepped into the shorts and pulled them up to his waist. The legs reached halfway down his shins. He pulled the waist up to his neck and his knees just slid into view. Boys pointed at them, shouting and laughing into each other's faces, and other boys who were still changing rushed to the scene, jumping up on the benches or parting the curtains to see through. And at the centre of it all, Billy, like a brave little clown, was busy trying to make them fit, and Sugden was looking at him as though it was his fault for being too small for them.

'Roll them down and don't be so foolish. You're too daft to laugh at, Casper.'

No one else thought so. Billy started to roll them down from his chest, each tuck shortening the legs and gathering the material round his waist in a floppy blue tyre.

'That'll do. Let's have you all out now.'

A Kestrel for a Knave by Barry Hines
(Penguin Books, 1969)

345

S OME OF US HAVE ALWAYS subscribed to Mark Twain's dictum that golf is 'a good walk spoiled'; others think differently ...

Seaside Golf
John Betjeman

How straight it flew, how long it flew,
    It clear'd the rutty track
And soaring, disappeared from view
    Beyond the bunker's back –
A glorious, sailing, bounding drive
That made me glad I was alive

And down the fairway, far along
    It glowed a lonely white;
I played an iron sure and strong
    And clipp'd it out of sight,
And spite of grassy banks between
I knew I'd find it on the green.

And so I did. It lay content
    Two paces from the pin;

Play Up and Play the Game

A steady putt and then it went
   Oh, most securely in.
The very turf rejoiced to see
That quite unprecedented three.

Ah! Seaweed smells from sandy caves
   And thyme and mist in whiffs,
In-coming tide, Atlantic waves
   Slapping the sunny cliffs,
Lark song and sea sounds in the air
And splendour, splendour everywhere.

from *Lasting the Course* by Peter Alliss
(Stanley Paul & Co., 1984)

O Tell Me the Truth About Love

So how does an Englishman differ in love from the rest? Eartha Kitt knows:

As you've guessed, I'm continental, romantic and
    sentimental,
I look on love as something of an art;
But I've found that nationalities
Have different formalities
When dealing with affairs of the heart.

Now the Spaniard needs a soft guitar
And a balcony to climb,
While the Portuguese need the breeze in the trees,
But an Englishman needs time.

The Italians long for an operatic song
Or a soft Sicilian rhyme,
While the French fall in love at the drop of a glove,
But an Englishman needs time.

He'll admit your attraction, but show no reaction,
His lips never part in a sigh;

England, Our England

What goes on in his breast is completely suppressed
By the weight of his old school tie.

The Viennese need a waltz by Strauss
Or a glockenspiel's sweet chime;
While the Dutch begin with a bottle of gin,
But an Englishman needs time.

A New Yorker's need is variety and speed,
But out west they're more sublime;
At a Hollywood ball they need nothing at all,
But an Englishman needs time.

He will meet you, maybe Monday night,
But unless he's quite unique,
He will call you up around Wednesday noon;
You get flowers Thursday week.

Though you have to wait, he may work up to a date,
But if he's really mad for you,
He will tenderly say, 'You look smashing today,'
And invite you to the zoo.

When you think it's all over, this mad Casanova
Arrives in a purposeful way,

But if he mentions sport, no, it's not what you thought,
It's to watch him play cricket all day.

Now in Persia, they need seven veils
For a sultan in his prime,
While an Eskimo needs a whole lot of snow,
But an Englishman needs time.

Now I love all those Englishmen,
But you must admit they are terribly ... Anglo-Saxon.
But after all is said and done,
And the battle is finally won,
Ladies, let's contemplate ...
Who wouldn't wait ...
For an Englishman who takes his time?

'An Englishman Needs Time' (1962),
Eartha Kitt (1927–)

L OVE MIGHT MAKE the world go round, but occasionally it can bring it to a grinding halt.

And yet, and yet, who would be without it? And you can always tell when love is in the air:

I can see from your utter misery, from your eagerness to misunderstand each other, and from your thoroughly bad temper, that this is the real thing.

Romanoff and Juliet (1956),
Peter Ustinov (1921–)

Sᴵʀ Jᴏʜɴ Bᴇᴛᴊᴇᴍᴀɴ seems to cover love in all its various moods and guises. I look for this couple every time I go to Bath:

> 'Let us not speak, for the love we bear one another –
>   Let us hold hands and look.'
> She, such a very ordinary little woman;
>   He, such a thumping crook;
> But both, for a moment, little lower than the angels
>   In the teashop's ingle-nook.

'In a Bath Teashop',
Sir John Betjeman (1906–84)

It has to be admitted that we English have sex on the brain, which is a very unsatisfactory place to have it.

Malcolm Muggeridge (1903–90)

356

D ID YOU EVER SEE Malcolm Muggeridge? Not the greatest looker. Perhaps Shakespeare was better endowed. With good looks, I mean. It is likely that his view will last longer than that of St Mugg. If you are in love, read Sonnet 116 to the object of your affections. Often.

Let me not to the marriage of true minds
Admit impediments. Love is not love
Which alters when it alteration finds,
Or bends with the remover to remove:
O, no! it is an ever-fixed mark,
That looks on tempests and is never shaken;
It is the star to every wandering bark,
Whose worth's unknown, although his height be taken.
Love's not Time's fool, though rosy lips and cheeks
Within his bending sickle's compass come;
Love alters not with his brief hours and weeks,
But bears it out even to the edge of doom.
If this be error and upon me proved,
I never writ, nor no man ever loved.

Sonnet 116 (1609),
William Shakespeare (1564–1616)

*When people say, 'You're breaking my heart,' they do
in fact mean that you're breaking their genitals.*

Jeffrey Barnard (1932–97)

DID YOU EVER SEE Jeffrey Barnard? He looked a lot like Malcolm Muggeridge. Christopher Marlowe could show them a thing or two. Was there ever such a shepherd as this? I do hope so. And I hope she went:

> Come live with me and be my Love,
> And we will all the pleasures prove
> That hills and valleys, dale and field,
> And all the craggy mountains yield.
>
> There will we sit upon the rocks
> And see the shepherds feed their flocks,
> By shallow rivers, to whose falls
> Melodious birds sing madrigals.
>
> There will I make thee beds of roses
> And a thousand fragrant posies,
> A cap of flowers, and a kirtle
> Embroider'd all with leaves of myrtle.
>
> A gown made of the finest wool,
> Which from our pretty lambs we pull,
> Fair linèd slippers for the cold,
> With buckles of the purest gold.

A belt of straw and ivy buds
With coral clasps and amber studs:
And if these pleasures may thee move,
Come live with me and be my Love.

Thy silver dishes for thy meat
As precious as the gods do eat,
Shall on an ivory table be
Prepared each day for thee and me.

The shepherd swains shall dance and sing
For thy delight each May-morning:
If these delights thy mind may move,
Then live with me and be my Love.

'The Passionate Shepherd to His Love' (*c*.1590),
Christopher Marlowe (1564–93)

NOT TO BE OUTDONE, Shakespeare, born in the same year as Marlowe, lays it on thickly, too, to equally good effect, one hopes:

> Shall I compare thee to a summer's day?
> Thou art more lovely and more temperate:
> Rough winds do shake the darling buds of May,
> And summer's lease hath all too short a date:
> Sometime too hot the eye of heaven shines,
> And often is his gold complexion dimm'd,
> And every fair from fair sometimes declines,
> By chance or nature's changing course untrimm'd;
> But thy eternal summer shall not fade,
> Nor lose possession of that fair thou ow'st,
> Nor shall Death brag thou wander'st in his shade,
> When in eternal lines to time thou grow'st,
> So long as men can breathe, or eyes can see,
> So long lives this, and this gives life to thee.

Sonnet 18 (1609),
William Shakespeare (1564–1616)

England, Our England

Sir John Betjeman expresses the sentiments of youth 350 years or so after Shakespeare. Oh, I do so remember those girls at the tennis club. But, alas, they won't remember me …

Miss J. Hunter Dunn, Miss J. Hunter Dunn,
Furnish'd and burnish'd by Aldershot sun,
What strenuous singles we played after tea,
We in the tournament – you against me!

Love-thirty, love-forty, oh! weakness of joy,
The speed of a swallow, the grace of a boy,
With carefullest carelessness, gaily you won,
I am weak from your loveliness, Joan Hunter Dunn.

Miss Joan Hunter Dunn, Miss Joan Hunter Dunn,
How mad I am, sad I am, glad that you won.
The warm-handled racket is back in its press,
But my shock-headed victor, she loves me no less.

Her father's euonymus shines as we walk,
And swing past the summer-house, buried in talk,
And cool the verandah that welcomes us in
To the six-o'clock news and a lime-juice and gin.

O Tell Me the Truth About Love

The scent of the conifers, sound of the bath,
The view from my bedroom of moss-dappled path,
As I struggle with double-end evening tie,
For we dance at the Golf Club, my victor and I.

On the floor of her bedroom lie blazer and shorts
And the cream-coloured walls are be-trophied with sports,
And westering, questioning settles the sun
On your low-leaded window, Miss Joan Hunter Dunn.

The Hillman is waiting, the light's in the hall,
The pictures of Egypt are bright on the wall,
My sweet, I am standing beside the oak stair
And there on the landing's the light on your hair.

By roads 'not adopted', by woodlanded ways,
She drove to the club in the late summer haze,
Into nine-o'clock Camberley, heavy with bells
And mushroomy, pine-woody, evergreen smells.

Miss Joan Hunter Dunn, Miss Joan Hunter Dunn,
I can hear from the car park the dance has begun.
Oh! full Surrey twilight! importunate band!
Oh! strongly adorable tennis-girl's hand!

England, Our England

Around us are Rovers and Austins afar,
Above us, the intimate roof of the car,
And here on my right is the girl of my choice,
With the tilt of her nose and the chime of her voice.

And the scent of her wrap, and the words never said,
And the ominous, ominous dancing ahead.
We sat in the car park till twenty to one
And now I'm engaged to Miss Joan Hunter Dunn.

'A Subaltern's Love Song' (1945),
Sir John Betjeman (1906–84)

HE NEVER DID WED HER. He married Penelope Chetwode instead. And a few years ago, I was having a cup of tea at a friend's house when there was a knock at the door. A lady stood there. An old lady. Well preserved. Collecting for the Red Cross. She shook her tin and smiled, and my friend handed over some change. The lady smiled again and retreated down the path. 'That,' said my friend, 'was Miss Joan Hunter Dunn.' She was no longer furnished and burnished by Aldershot sun. Just rather sweet.

And then there was the one that Betjeman wanted to avoid like the plague:

> Keep me from Thelma's sister Pearl!
> She puts my senses in a whirl,
> Weakens my knees and keeps me waiting
> Until my heart stops palpitating.
>
> The debs may turn disdainful backs
> On Pearl's uncouth mechanic slacks,
> And outraged see the fire that lies
> And smoulders in her long-lashed eyes.
>
> Have they such weather-freckled features,
> The smooth, sophisticated creatures?

Ah, not to them such limbs belong,
Such animal movements sure and strong,

Such arms to take a man and press
In agricultural caress
His head to hers, and hold him there
Deep buried in her chestnut hair.

God shrive me from this morning lust
For supple farm girls: if you must,
Send the cold daughter of an earl –
But spare me Thelma's sister Pearl!

'Agricultural Caress',
Sir John Betjeman (1906–84)

AND IF ALL ELSE FAILS, you can always go to a singles'
club. Or surf the Net. Or join a dancing class ...

My neighbour, Mrs Fanshaw, is portly-plump and gay,
She must be over sixty-seven, if she is a day.
You might have thought her life was dull,
It's one long whirl instead.
I asked her all about it, and this is what she said:

I've joined an Olde Thyme Dance Club, the trouble is that there
Are too many ladies over, and no gentlemen to spare.
It seems a shame, it's not the same,
But still it has to be,
Some ladies have to dance together,
One of them is me.

Stately as a galleon, I sail across the floor,
Doing the Military Two-Step, as in the days of yore.
I dance with Mrs Tiverton; she's light on her feet, in spite
Of turning the scale at fourteen stone, and being of medium
    height.
So gay the band,
So giddy the sight,
Full evening dress is a must,

But the zest goes out of a beautiful waltz
When you dance it bust to bust.

So, stately as two galleons, we sail across the floor,
Doing the Valse Valeta as in the days of yore.
The gent is Mrs Tiverton, I am her lady fair,
She bows to me ever so nicely and I curtsey to her with care.
So gay the band,
So giddy the sight,
But it's not the same in the end
For a lady is never a gentleman, though
She may be your bosom friend.

So, stately as a galleon, I sail across the floor,
Doing the dear old Lancers, as in the days of yore.
I'm led by Mrs Tiverton, she swings me round and round,
And though she manoeuvres me wonderfully well
I never get off the ground.
So gay the band,
So giddy the sight,
I try not to get depressed.
And it's done me a power of good to explode,
And get this lot off my chest.

'Stately as a Galleon' (1978),
Joyce Grenfell (1910–79)

W<small>E ALL TRY TO UNDERSTAND IT</small>. Try not to fall foul of it. Try to keep our emotions in control. And we all fail. Like humour, if you analyse love, it just doesn't stand up to it.

Some say love's a little boy,
And some say it's a bird,
Some say it makes the world go round,
And some say that's absurd,
And when I asked the man next door,
Who looked as if he knew,
His wife got very cross indeed,
And said it wouldn't do.

Does it look like a pair of pyjamas,
Or the ham in a temperance hotel?
Does its odour remind one of llamas,
Or has it a comforting smell?
Is it prickly to touch as a hedge is,
Or soft as eiderdown fluff?
Is it sharp or quite smooth at the edges?
O tell me the truth about love.

Our history books refer to it
In cryptic little notes,

It's quite a common topic on
The Transatlantic boats;
I've found the subject mentioned in
Accounts of suicides,
And even seen it scribbled on
The backs of railway guides.

Does it howl like a hungry Alsatian,
Or boom like a military band?
Could one give a first-rate imitation
On a saw or a Steinway grand?
Is its singing at parties a riot?
Does it only like classical stuff?
Will it stop when one wants to be quiet?
O tell me the truth about love.

I looked inside the summer-house;
It wasn't ever there:
I tried the Thames at Maidenhead,
And Brighton's bracing air.
I don't know what the blackbird sang,
Or what the tulip said;
But it wasn't in the chicken-run,
Or underneath the bed.

O Tell Me the Truth About Love

Can it pull extraordinary faces?
Is it usually sick on a swing?
Does it spend all its time at the races,
Or fiddling with pieces of string?
Has it views of its own about money?
Does it think Patriotism enough?
Are its stories vulgar but funny?
O tell me the truth about love.

When it comes, will it come without warning
Just as I'm picking my nose?
Will it knock on my door in the morning,
Or tread in the bus on my shoes?
Will it come like a change in the weather?
Will its greeting be courteous or rough?
Will it alter my life altogether?
O tell me the truth about love.

'O Tell Me the Truth About Love' (1937),
W. H. Auden (1907–73)

Hopping the Twig

In
Loving
Memory

I'M SORRY TO END ON a sad note; but in times of death one needs solace. And humour. And if we are smiled on, we have old age to look forward to before hopping the twig. This seems to be the favourite poem of anyone preparing to leave middle age behind for something more scary:

When I am an old woman I shall wear purple
With a red hat which doesn't go, and doesn't suit me.
And I shall spend my pension on brandy and summer gloves
And satin sandals, and say we've no money for butter.
I shall sit down on the pavement when I'm tired
And gobble up samples in shops and press alarm bells
And run my stick along the public railings
And make up for the sobriety of my youth.
I shall go out in my slippers in the rain
And pick the flowers in other people's gardens
And learn to spit.

You can wear terrible shirts and grow more fat
And eat three pounds of sausages at a go
Or only bread and pickle for a week
And hoard pens and pencils and beermats and things in boxes.

But now we must have clothes that keep us dry
And pay our rent and not swear in the street
And set a good example for the children.
We must have friends to dinner and read the papers.

But maybe I ought to practise a little now?
So people who know me are not too shocked and surprised
When suddenly I am old, and start to wear purple.

'Warning' (1974),
Jenny Joseph (1932–)

I do get told off for rushing round to much. For working too
hard. But then I discovered these lines in *A Shropshire Lad*
and I understood why . . .

Clay lies still, but blood's a rover;
Breath's a ware that will not keep.
Up, lad; when the journey's over
There'll be time enough to sleep.

A Shropshire Lad, 1896
A. E. Houseman 1859–1936

Who killed Cock Robin?
I, said the Sparrow,
With my bow and arrow,
I killed Cock Robin.

Who saw him die?
I, said the Fly,
With my little eye,
I saw him die.

Who caught his blood?
I, said the Fish,
With my little dish,
I caught his blood.

Who'll make his shroud?
I, said the Beetle,
With my thread and needle,
I'll make the shroud.

Who'll dig his grave?
I, said the Owl,

With my pick and shovel,
I'll dig his grave.

Who'll be the parson?
I, said the Rook,
With my little book,
I'll be the parson.

Who'll be the clerk?
I, said the Lark,
If it's not in the dark,
I'll be the clerk.

Who'll carry the link?
I, said the Linnet,
I'll fetch it in a minute,
I'll carry the link.

Who'll be the chief mourner?
I, said the Dove,
I mourn for my love,
I'll be chief mourner.

Who'll carry the coffin?
I, said the Kite,

Hopping the Twig

If it's not through the night,
I'll carry the coffin.

Who'll bear the pall?
We, said the Wren,
Both the Cock and the Hen,
We'll bear the pall.

Who'll sing a psalm?
I, said the Thrush,
As she sat on a bush,
I'll sing a psalm.

Who'll toll the bell?
I, said the Bull,
Because I can pull,
So, Cock Robin, farewell.

All the birds of the air
Fell a-sighing and a-sobbing,
When they heard the bell toll
For poor Cock Robin.

'Cock Robin' (date unknown), Anon.

The English find ill-health not only interesting but respectable, and often experience death in the effort to avoid a fuss.

Pen to Paper (1961),
Pamela Frankau (1908–67)

I N SPITE OF BEING INTRODUCED to it by morbid nursery rhymes, death can still be puzzling to small children, as Dirk Bogarde recalls in his childhood memoir:

It really wasn't the sort of morning on which rotten things are supposed to happen.

All the way up from the little iron gate at the bottom of Great Meadow the larks were singing like anything. The sun was hot, and the leaves on the elder and ash at the edge of the gully had just started to turn yellowy-goldish, because it was going to be September in a minute although you would hardly have known it, it was so beautiful.

The high grasses were full of crickets and grasshoppers, and the field curved away up towards the sky, soft and smooth and fawn as a deer's back. Only very little clouds drifted in high above from the sea at Cuckmere and sort of got melted away by the warm breeze which came in the other way from the Weald.

We didn't really know much about the witch. We had spoken to her once, years ago, with all her cats round her. She had been quite nice and showed us a sort of shell thing with *Bombay* written on it, which is a town in India, because we had given her a bit of help with some wood for her fire. But that was all, and she didn't put a spell on us, as far as we knew, although my sister did get the measles a bit later on and I didn't, which was jolly lucky for me. But that was the only time we'd been really close. I mean, we never spoke again or anything like that.

We sometimes used to see her hurrying along, shoulders all hunched up in a very witchy way, and her old black felt hat pulled down right to her eyes looking exactly like half an egg, which is why we called her Eggshell, although we actually knew that her real name was Nellie Wardle. She never spoke to us, or even looked, and we didn't dare speak to her in case of something funny happening. You couldn't be sure with witches. She just went on past, wagging her head from side to side and muttering awful-sounding things to herself in her long black draggly coat which was really quite green if you saw it in the sunlight, which we didn't often because she mostly came out at dusk. With the bats. Witches do.

We never went back to the caravan on Red Barn Hill where she lived with all those cats, because it was a pretty creepy, lonely sort of place, and if you had been 'spelled' there, no one would ever have known about it.

But sometimes we saw her on Fridays when Fred the Fish drove in from Newhaven in his shiny little Morris van. We'd be able to see her quite close to, because after everyone had bought what they wanted, and Fred was clearing up his boxes and the big brass scales, she used to get a fat parcel of fish heads and skin and stuff wrapped up in newspaper which he gave her for her cats.

And that's how we knew that she was dead.

This Friday he was scraping the guts and so on into a bucket, and I was putting our herrings into the red and black shopping-bag, and I said to him, 'Are you saving all those bits for Mrs Wardle's cats?'

'No. No more I don't. She's gorn.' And he went on wiping his chopping-board.

My sister looked very shocked and said, 'Gorn where?' Which would have got her a box on the ears if Lally had heard her.

He just shrugged and said, 'Gorn,' again, but he didn't know where for certain.

'There's two places, ain't there?' he said. 'There's your Heaven and there's your Hell. Who can tell where she's skipped to?'

My sister looked quite white and said, 'There's the other place too … the Purgatory place, isn't there?'

He wrung out his cloth, squeezed it quite dry and said that was *Life*. Not death. And then we knew that she was dead. Of course, we had really known as soon as he had said, 'Gorn.' I mean we knew it wasn't to Seaford or Hastings or somewhere, but much worse. And further.

But dead. It seemed very final, sort of. We were quite miserable when we went across to Baker's the confectioner's to get Lally her Fry's chocolate bar and us our Sherbert Dabs. Miss Annie said, 'Yes, poor soul, didn't you know? Jack Diplock found her on the path with all her cats sitting round her, dead as the Dodo.' She said she reckoned she'd gorn just in time to get ready for the haunting at the end of October.

Great Meadow (1992),
Dirk Bogarde (1921–99)

A ND THEN THERE ARE the poems of solace, which I include here with no further introduction. They speak for
themselves, and hopefully for those who grieve.

Stop all the clocks, cut off the telephone,
Prevent the dog from barking with a juicy bone,
Silence the pianos and with muffled drum
Bring out the coffin, let the mourners come.

Let aeroplanes circle moaning overhead,
Scribbling on the sky the message 'He is dead.'
Put crêpe bows round the white necks of the public doves,
Let the traffic policemen wear black cotton gloves.

He was my North, my South, my East and West,
My working week and my Sunday rest,
My noon, my midnight, my talk, my song;
I thought that love would last for ever: I was wrong.

The stars are not wanted now: put out every one;
Pack up the moon and dismantle the sun;
Pour away the ocean and sweep up the wood.
For nothing now can ever come to any good.

'Funeral Blues' (1936), W. H. Auden (1907–73)

Do not stand at my grave and weep;
I am not there. I do not sleep.
I am a thousand winds that blow
I am the diamond glints on snow.
I am the sunlight on ripened grain.
I am the gentle autumn rain.
When you awaken in the morning's hush
I am the swift uplifting rush
Of quiet birds in circled flight.
I am the soft stars that shine at night.
Do not stand at my grave and cry;
I am not there. I did not die.

'Do not stand at my grave and weep' (date unknown),
Mary Elizabeth Frye (1904–2004)*

* Frye is believed to be the author, but this is not certain.

Remember me when I am gone away,
 Gone far away into the silent land;
 When you can no more hold me by the hand,
Nor I half turn to go yet turning stay.
Remember me when no more day by day
 You tell me of our future that you planned:
 Only remember me; you understand
It will be late to counsel then or pray.
Yet if you should forget me for a while
 And afterwards remember, do not grieve:
 For if the darkness and corruption leave
 A vestige of the thoughts that once I had,
Better by far you should forget and smile
 Than that you should remember and be sad.

'Remember' (1862),
Christina Rossetti (1830–94)

In Flanders fields the poppies blow
Between the crosses, row on row,
    That mark our place; and in the sky
    The larks, still bravely singing, fly
Scarce heard amid the guns below.

We are the Dead. Short days ago
We lived, felt dawn, saw sunset glow,
    Loved and were loved, and now we lie
    In Flanders fields.

Take up our quarrel with the foe:
To you from failing hands we throw
    The torch; be yours to hold it high.
    If ye break faith with us who die
We shall not sleep, though poppies grow
    In Flanders fields.

'In Flanders Fields' (1915),
John McCrae (1872–1918)

If I should die, think only this of me:
   That there's some corner of a foreign field
That is for ever England. There shall be
   In that rich earth a richer dust concealed;
A dust whom England bore, shaped, made aware,
   Gave, once, her flowers to love, her ways to roam,
A body of England's, breathing English air,
   Washed by the rivers, blest by suns of home.

And think, this heart, all evil shed away,
   A pulse in the eternal mind, no less
      Gives somewhere back the thoughts by England given;
Her sights and sounds; dreams happy as her day;
   And laughter, learnt of friends; and gentleness,
      In hearts at peace, under an English heaven.

'The Soldier' (1914),
Rupert Brooke (1887–1915)

389

S HAKESPEARE WROTE HIS FAMOUS speech about the seven
ages of man. All that mewling and puking and unwillingly
to school stuff. What he did not refer to were the other seven
ages of man: weddings, christenings, anniversaries, divorces,
remarriages, widowhood and memorial services. The memorial
service is there to remind those of us who are left behind not
to take things too much for granted. Roy Strong is a regular at-
tender.

The late Lady Hartwell once said to me: 'Remember, Roy, life
after the age of thirty-five is one long memorial service.'
More than a decade on I went to her memorial service, one
remarkable for its flowers and for the absence of any eulo-
gistic address. It was vividly reflective of her dislike of hum-
bug and her innate modesty, not easily perceived on first
encounter.

Another service, also at St Margaret's, Westminster, which
went minus address was for Lord Hood. It brings to mind a
conversation I overheard soon afterwards between what
must have been two full-time memorial-service-goers: 'Oh,
you should have gone instead to Rhoda Birley's. It had spe-
cially composed music and John Betjeman chose the hymns.'
Did the person who muttered these words, I've often wondered, scour the Court page of *The Times*, deciding which

service would be the aesthetic hit of the day?

I must confess to a certain drollery towards it all. There can be no doubt, however, that there has been a vast multiplication in the practice of holding memorial or thanksgiving services in the last few years. The funerals of public figures, unlike a century ago, have become private events and the necessary public expression of grief, memory and celebration has been transferred to the memorial service.

In London four churches virtually monopolise the industry: St Margaret's (mainly political), St Paul's, Covent Garden (theatre and the arts), St Martin-in-the-Fields, and St James's, Piccadilly (taking in what they can). Having lately gone to so many, I am aware that most people have a set of 'black' tucked away in their wardrobes; it is one of the few occasions when women are relatively oblivious to fashion, and old clothes are the norm.

The memorial service is an event neatly timed within an ordered day not to interfere with the morning's work, nor upset any appointment for luncheon at one. It is a muted midday gathering of the establishment and *le monde* to commemorate a gap in its ranks. Sometimes they are wonderful, sometimes they fall flat, and sometimes something goes wrong.

Who would ever have thought that the late Marie Rambert's service would have been plagued from start to finish by the noise of a barrel organ outside in the piazza? Or that, as we sat down, the pew would collapse. How she would have loved it! Sometimes an address can go awry. At a service for Benedict Nicolson, Lord Clark, normally an impeccable eulogiser, suddenly launched into an attack on the Bloomsbury Group.

Theatrical services tend to be memorable for everyone involved, including the congregation. Sir Lewis Casson's took place in Westminster Abbey, and I shall always remember the distant echoing voices of the choir singing of paradise, and the sight of Sybil Thorndike in the procession, all in white, smiling and happy like a bride on her wedding day.

Oliver Messel's service brought glimpses of the heroines of one's youth, Evelyn Laye and Dorothy Dickson. But it was notable for the finest memorial address I have ever heard, delivered extempore, it seemed, by Dame Ninette de Valois. A worthier epitaph he could never have wished for than her recollection of an ancient Russian who remarked on seeing his *Sleeping Beauty* in Leningrad, 'Tchaikovsky and Petipa should have been alive to have seen this!'

Cecil Beaton's service, at which I was an usher, was rather flat by comparison. How irritated he would have been to see the pews filling up with so many people I recall him categorising as 'ghastly'. One of the drawbacks of the memorial service is that it is open house, which means perhaps that there is still something to be said for the funeral. If Beaton's memorial service misfired, his funeral was a triumph. It was extraordinary to walk up to the church with flowers laid on either side of the path, including tributes from so many of his goddesses – Irene Worth, Garbo and, most typical of all, a floral crown from the inimitable Lady Diana Cooper. In this instance I'm glad I went to both.

Fortunately the Church of England still offers its hospitality, its liturgy and its hymns in memory of the agnostic or inactive believer. I never feel happy at those secular gatherings. Bare addresses, perhaps a reading or two, a piece of music and then straight on to the glass of plonk and the chatter. But then it never is comforting to have the vision of eternity removed.

Strong Points (1985),
Sir Roy Strong (1935–)

THE LAST WORD OF ALL goes to England's greatest national hero. The man who saved us from being invaded by those peculiar people across the Channel.

He stands for everything we like to think we are: good-mannered, slow to anger, stoic, loyal, honest, fair, trustworthy and almost always right. Horatio, Lord Nelson wrote out this prayer the night before the Battle of Trafalgar. A battle which he won for his country, but at the cost of his own life. We should all, in our own little battles for England, remember his sentiments and glow with pride.

It is allowed. Occasionally.

May the Great God, whom I worship, grant to my Country and for the benefit of Europe in general a great and glorious victory; and may no misconduct in anyone tarnish it; and may humanity after Victory be the predominant feature of the British Fleet. For myself, individually, I commit my life to Him who made me, and may His blessing light upon my endeavours for serving my Country faithfully. To Him I resign myself and the just cause which is entrusted me to defend.

Amen. Amen. Amen.

Diary entry on the eve of the Battle of Trafalgar (21 October 1805),
Horatio, Lord Nelson (1758–1805)

Acknowledgements

'Portraits from Memory' by Bertrand Russell – Used with kind permission.

'Tea With the Queen' by Unity Hall & Ingrid Seward. Used by kind permission of Ingrid Seward.

'Yorkshire's Great Houses' by Sir Thomas Ingilby Bart. Used by kind permission of Country Publications Limited.

'There Are Bad Times Just Around The Corner' by Noel Coward. Copyright © NC Aventales AG. Permission to reprint has been kindly provided by: Methuen Drama, an imprint of A&C Black Publishers. And, Copyright agent: Alan Brodie Representation Ltd. 6th floor, Fairgate House, 78 New Oxford Street, London WC1A 1HB, info@alanbrodie.com

'A Song of Patriotic Prejudice' reproduced by permission of the Estates of Michael Flanders & Donald Swann 2007. Any use of Flanders & Swann material, large or small,